Death of a Myth

KYLE HASELDEN

Death of a Myth

NEW LOCUS FOR SPANISH AMERICAN FAITH

Friendship Press   New York

Library of Congress Catalog Card Number: 64-10997

To Francis A. Castillos

Contents

Part Three: Receiving from Spanish Americans

✒ PREFACE

Titling a book dealing with the Spanish American–Anglo-Protestant encounter in the United States poses many difficulties. In the first place, we are thinking of multiple groups of people who are loosely tied together by one common characteristic: an ancient and variously modified cultural heritage from medieval Spain. Except for this heritage, Spanish Americans are a heterogeneous people whose differences defy general classification. Second, our study is limited to the continental United States, excluding the Commonwealth of Puerto Rico and dealing only with those Puerto Ricans who have come from the island to the mainland. Protestantism on the island is another story that must be told elsewhere. Third, it is difficult—in fact, impossible—to give a universally acceptable title to such a diverse ethnic group. When in Chapter 1 we explore their identities and diversities and seek a nomenclature for them, we shall see why there is no adequate collective name for the members of this ethnic minority and why we must arbitrarily adopt the one we think most fitting. We are therefore using the phrase "Spanish American," noting the inadequacy as well as the appropriateness of this term. Fourth, we are exploring the meeting of Spanish Americans and Anglo-Protestantism in the United States. We must make sure that neither the substance of this book nor its title implies a kind of *noblesse oblige* on the part of Anglo-Protestants and a passive acceptance and gratitude on the part of Spanish Americans who join Protestant churches. The benefits of the encounter flow both ways.

Most important, we must not encourage the popular but erroneous assumption that the Protestant mission to Spanish Americans is a crude effort to make Protestants out of a people who are loyally and predominantly Roman Catholic. This assumption reflects an ignorance of the facts about Spanish Americans, who largely practice a noninstitutional religion and who are devout, formal Roman Catholics in minority numbers. The assumption that all Spanish Americans are Roman Catholic and that Protestantism and Spanish American culture and personality are incompatible is a myth that must be repudiated in the Spanish American but particularly in the Anglo-American mind. We therefore use *Death of a Myth* as our title, for one of the primary purposes of this study is to introduce Anglo-Protestants and Spanish Americans in the continental United States to each other in a way that will destroy the myth. The ignorance with which we are dealing, and which we are seeking to remove, is largely an Anglo-American ignorance. Therefore this study is addressed first to the Anglo-Protestant and second to the Spanish American Protestant.

If this work generates awareness in both ethnic groups, if it stimulates communication between the two, if it helps to discover and provide a new locus for Spanish American faith, if it makes for that Christian oneness that eliminates the kinds of distinctions our study requires, the time and thought given to it will have been well spent.

For some of the data used in this study I am indebted to Bertha Blair, Anne O. Lively, and Glen W. Trimble for an unpublished report they produced for the Home Missions Research Unit of the Division of Home Missions of the National Council of the Churches of Christ in the United States of America. I express my gratitude to them and request that the uses to which I have put some of their materials be charged solely to me.

—KYLE HASELDEN

PART ONE

Understanding Spanish Americans

. . . *The Caribbean Nursery*

From its earliest precolonial days to the present,
the history of the United States is a chronicle of immigrants.
It is a story of successive waves of newcomers who for a
variety of reasons left their homes, braved uncertainty, en-
dured hardship, and took their chances on a better life in a
new world. The saga of these strangers reaches into antiquity
and includes the Indian, whose coming to the central part
of North America occurred so long ago and is so shrouded
in obscurity that we think of him as the only native American. It includes those people who came voluntarily to this
mid-continent—Spanish, British, French, Dutch, German,
Irish, Polish, Italian, and, more recently, Mexican, Puerto
Rican, and Cuban. The annals of the immigrants to the
United States—sometimes romantic and heroic, sometimes
shameful and tragic—also tell the story of those Americans
who became a part of this history unwillingly: the Negroes,
whose ancestors were brought here as slaves, and those Spanish Americans whose forebears were made a part of this country by military conquest. From the first Indian to the latest
Cuban refugee we Americans are, without exception, a people whose odysseys began a long time ago in faraway lands.

If we are to understand Spanish Americans—a combination of immigrants—we must know where they come from and who they are. So, first, we shall have a swift review of early American history. Everyone knows that the Indian is the oldest American, but the biases of our history books, oriented toward England, conceal the fact that the Spanish American is second oldest. And, since most Spanish Americans are a Spanish-Indian combination of races and cultures, they can rightly claim that through one of their lines—the Indian—they were here before anyone else, and through the other line—the Spanish—they pressed the first stamp of their color and their culture upon this continent one hundred years before any other white man attempted to do so. No one can say to them that if they don't like it here they can go back to where they came from. The Spanish Americans were here first.

To be correct, we must say that the American part of the Spanish American story in the northern half of the Western Hemisphere began with the Indian in an antiquity now lost to history. The Spanish part of this drama opened in the Caribbean in the closing years of the fifteenth century. On October 12, 1492, after more than two months in voyage, Christopher Columbus, an Italian sailing under Spanish auspices, landed on a small island of the Bahamas—possibly San Salvador—southeast of Florida. From this island Columbus sailed on Sunday, October 28, along the coast of Cuba, which he called "the most beautiful land human eyes have ever seen." He landed at Haiti, where in the same year he left men to make the first white settlement in the new world. On his second voyage, in 1493, Columbus discovered Puerto Rico, which he named San Juan Bautista (St. John the Baptist), a name preserved today in the commonwealth's capital city. Cuba and Puerto Rico received the first immigrants from Europe and now contribute the most recent immigrants to the United States. They play a primary and central role in the Spanish American story.

Fifteen years after the discovery of Puerto Rico, in 1508, one of the young Spanish officers who had traveled with Columbus, Juan Ponce de León, returned to the island to settle it for the Spanish, becoming its first governor in 1510. The Spanish found there roughly thirty thousand Arawak Indians—a peace loving, gentle tribe—and a sprinkling of the more warlike Caribs. The culture of the Arawaks was relatively advanced, especially their stone sculpture, which ranks with any found in the new world. But the aggressive Spaniards soon subdued the docile Arawaks and fastened on the island a severe colonialism that was to last for nearly four hundred years. In 1511, the Spaniards brought the first Negro slaves from Africa to Puerto Rico and established in the island the beginnings of three centuries of traffic in human beings. Parallel events developed in Cuba, the island that Columbus had found so beautiful as he passed it. In 1511, the Spaniard, Diego Velásquez, conquered the Arawaks in Cuba and with three hundred men established the first colony in the island. He, too, like Ponce de León, imported Negro slaves from Africa.

. . .   *A Multiple Legacy*

We may mark these dates and these islands as the beginning of a multiple racial blending: Europeans and Indians, producing mestizos; Negroes and Indians, producing sambos; Europeans and Negroes, producing mulattoes. Since Spanish women were always scarce in the islands, and since Spaniards had few of the racial scruples English colonists pretended to have, the mixing of the races in every possible combination was free, open, and general. What has been said of Puerto Rico could be said with minor modifications of Cuba: "The bloodstreams of all these migrants fused to make the Puerto Rican of today. He is not a Negro, though 20 per cent of the population is Negro. He is not an Indian, yet the golden skin, the high cheek-bones, the aquiline nose, the gentleness and hospitality of the Indians are a common trait all over the island. He is not a Spaniard, yet he may have the blond hair of Northern Spain and the pure white skin of Barcelona." [1] In these islands Indians and Spaniards have now largely disappeared and the Negro population is rapidly declining. In 1960, the Negro population in Puerto Rico was 20 per cent. In 1899, according to a census of the island taken by the United States Army, the Negroes constituted 38 per cent of the population. The United States Army may have had a more inclusive definition of "Negro" than modern censuses. The amalgamating process still has a long way to go in removing racial distinctions or the marks of a racially distinct ancestry, but the process continues.

We shall see the Indian playing a larger role in the building of a new racial stock when we meet the Mexican and the Hispano, but it is highly improbable that after these 450 years of racial crosscurrents many Spanish Americans are genetically purely European in their ancestry. Today some Spanish Americans in New Mexico, California, Colorado, Texas, and Arizona prefer the title "Spanish colonials" or the more recent title "Hispanos." But most of the old Spanish families in the Southwest of the United States are mestizos, too. When their Spanish ancestors came to the northwestern regions of New Spain—the Spanish viceroyalty in North America—three hundred years ago, they married Indian women. Their children spoke Spanish, preserved Spanish customs, and until this day live in an isolation that has brought seventeenth century Spanish culture into the twentieth century. But most of them did not escape the racial blending. In the light of the facts, a Spanish American of pure Spanish ancestry is a rarity. Carey McWilliams in *North from Mexico* writes: "Not more than three hundred thousand Spaniards came to the Americas in the three

---

[1] Gruber, Ruth. *Puerto Rico: Island of Promise*, p. 26. New York: Hill and Wang, 1960.

colonial centuries and many of these, of course, came only for short periods and later returned. . . . It is doubtful if more than fifty thousand Spanish-born persons have resided in the United States at any one period from 1820 to the present time." [2]

If this relatively small group of Spanish immigrants had been race conscious, their racial purity—such as it was— might have been preserved; but since this was not the case, it is probable that most Spanish Americans have Indian ancestors and that some of them have Negro as well as white forebears. In a Protestant Episcopal conference on Latin-American relations in the southwestern United States, Ralph Estrada, former president of Alianza Hispano-Americana (a regional organization of the Southwest dedicated to improving the status of Mexican Americans), said, "However, I sincerely believe that the Spaniard who came into this land [New Spain] has become a part of the Indian society he once conquered and no longer can be distinguished from that society. Where once we spoke of Spanish-American, we must now say Mexican-American, for only in the culture of Mexico and not of Spain do we in the United States share a common heritage." [3]

The multiple legacy inherited by Mexicans, Hispanos, Puerto Ricans, and Cubans from the crossbreeding that began in the West Indies was a blending of cultures as well as races. The Spanish culture, more advanced and aggressive than any it met in the islands of the new world, was soon dominant over less vigorous, indigenous cultures. But the extent and intensity of that domination varied according to the virility of the peoples whom it subdued and the state of

---

[2] McWilliams, Carey. *North from Mexico: The Spanish-Speaking People of the United States*, p. 20. Philadelphia and New York: J. B. Lippincott Co., 1949.

[3] *Summary of Conference on Latin-American Relations in the Southwestern United States*, p. 13. Division of Racial Minorities, The National Council of the Protestant Episcopal Church, New York, 1959.

the civilization it met. Something was given by the Spanish immigrants to the newly developing race and culture, but something was also contributed by the Indian. Even in such a country as Puerto Rico, where the number of Indians was small and their resistance to Spanish advances weak, subtle traces of the older American culture remain. For example, the island of the Arawaks was called Borinquén, and they were known as Borinqueños. The Arawak Indians are gone, but the name Borinqueños remains as a popular title for Puerto Ricans and the national anthem of the commonwealth is known as "La Borinqueña." Numerous other words that made their way from Indian languages into the English by way of Spanish are testimony to the impact of the native culture upon the newcomers.

When the Spaniards moved from the periphery of Indian culture to its center in Mexico, they discovered a civilization in many ways equal and in some ways superior to their own. "What Columbus discovered, of course, were islands of America where flourished a culture whose principal center was as large (and as beautiful) as Venice, whose philosophy and mathematics contained some precepts as profound as those of the Greeks, and whose knowledge of astronomy was as accurate as that of European scientists. It is not likely that members of this culture would admit that Columbus had 'discovered' anything." [4] Long before the Spaniards arrived, the Aztecs had an architecture, an accurate calendar, a zero-including system of mathematics, a theology, an astronomy, a military development, and a sway of empire that in these respects equated their civilization with that of the old world. Militarily and culturally the Spaniards conquered these people, but the invading Spaniards in turn were conquered by many aspects of the Aztec civilization.

[4] From A Short History of Mexico, by J. Patrick McHenry. Copyright, 1962, by J. Patrick McHenry. Reprinted by permission of Doubleday and Co., Inc.

What issued from the clashing and the eventual blending of these two forces was a true Spanish-Indian culture. When we think today of the contributions of the Spanish Americans to the culture of the United States, we are thinking in part of an Aztec contribution that came to this country through the Spanish American line. The mixture of genes, ideologies, and customs was thorough.

Wherever the Spaniards went they took their Roman Catholic religion with them, whether they were deeply religious or not. It is a prejudiced view, and an erroneous one, to say that the English Pilgrims came to this country for God and the Spaniards came solely for gold. The Spaniards did come for gold, for the material riches they expected to find and, in some cases, did find in the new world. But they did not come for gold only. It is instructive to note, on the contrary, how consistently the Spanish explorers, in obedience to Pope Alexander VI, claimed new land for God and the church as well as for Spain, how promptly they brought priests to the new world for the conversion of the natives, and how soon an ecclesiastical structure was established in colonized areas. On his fourth voyage, Columbus brought priests with him and, according to Roman Catholic records, even established a convent in Santo Domingo. In 1522, Hernando Cortés received twelve Franciscan friars in Mexico City, falling on his knees and, to the astonishment of the Indians, kissing the hems of their dirty, tattered robes. In 1518, the Diocese of all Cuba was established in Baruca by Pope Leo X. With rare exception, the attitude of the early Roman Catholic missionaries toward the Indian aborigines was one that accepted the Indian as a child of God, sought his conversion to Christianity, dealt mercifully with him, and tried to protect him from brutal exploitation by his Spanish conquerors.

The façade of Roman Catholicism, as well as many of its redemptive values, was impressed upon all the lands taken by the Spanish invaders. One need only read the names given by the Spaniards to the places they conquered and settled, or count the numerous ancient churches in the region covered by New Spain, to see that this is true. But the blending of cultures, the modification of one civilization by the other, had its effect upon religion as upon everything else. Outwardly, the lands settled by the Spanish were Roman Catholic at the end of the three centuries of colonization. Inwardly—in the beliefs and practices of the great masses of the people—the religion of New Spain was a mixture of Christianity and the superstitions and primitive customs of the native Indians. To this mixture was added in some places the animism and voodooism imported by Negro slaves from Africa. Under the impact of the acculturating forces at work in all the vast Spanish-invaded area, there developed a conglomerate religion that had all the externalities of Roman Catholicism. But this Catholicism, corrupted by indigenous religions and exchanging its sacrificial spirit for the power lost by the Spanish rulers, failed—as we see later in more detail—the moral and spiritual needs of the people. Indeed, the church adopted the abusive role of the conquistadores and despoiled rather than served the people. The result was that many of the people in New Spain repudiated Christianity altogether, many were Roman Catholic in name only, and many practiced a religion that was sometimes Roman Catholic, sometimes pagan. The church conquered and was conquered by the new world.

.   .   .   *The Spreading Fan*

From their bases in the Caribbean the venturesome Spaniards sent exploratory and colonizing parties south, west, and north in a vast semicircle. They landed with a splash in the middle of the Caribbean and almost immediately sent rippling waves of conquest and colonization to every shore touched by that sea. Ponce de León, searching for the legendary fountain of youth, sailed from Puerto Rico and on March 27, 1513, discovered the Florida mainland, landing north of the present site of St. Augustine on April 2. His mission failed, and on a subsequent invasion of Florida he was repulsed by fierce Indian tribes and was mortally wounded. But the mainland had been challenged, and by 1565, the Spanish invaders had established the first European colony within the territory that later comprised the original United States.

Six years after Ponce de León discovered Florida, Diego Velásquez, the governor of Cuba, sent Hernando Cortés, with 110 mariners, 555 soldiers, and 16 horses, to invade and explore what is now Mexico. They landed at a site that they named Veracruz, lost thirty men to the ravages of sickness, boldly sank their ships, and proceeded inland to the Aztec capital, Tenochtitlán, site of the present Mexico City. With his superiority of arms and with brutality and cunning, Cortés and his men defeated the Aztec forces sent against them, captured the emperor, Montezuma, and by holding him prisoner put all of Mexico under their rule. The rebellion of the Aztecs against their conquerors continued for months, but through intrigue, brute force, and cunning, Cortés reduced the proud Indians to complete subjection. Despite his cruelty, vanity, and ambition, Cortés must be credited with establishing in the conquered land a government that made possible the coexistence and eventually the commingling of Spaniards and Indians, assuring an interpenetration of the two cultures and peoples during the following 450 years.

From central Mexico such explorers as Francisco Vásquez de Coronado—whose forays took him into present day California, Arizona, New Mexico, Texas, Oklahoma, and western Kansas—pushed the territorial claims of Spain and spread the Spanish influence through all of that region now known as the southwestern United States. When the younger English nation pushed west it found in its path to the Pacific an established Spanish-Indian civilization thinly spread north and west of the Rio Grande over an area as large as all of the United States east of the Mississippi River. "In 1810 the population of Mexico [including the northern region] was roughly estimated to be 6,000,000 people—40,000 Spaniards, 1,000,000 Creoles [American born descendants of Spanish parents], 3,500,000 pure-blooded Indians, and 1,500,-000 mestizos. From this it can be seen that the Spaniards were a small ruling minority—an oligarchy—whom the Creoles bitterly resented and the Indians and mestizos hated." [5] By this date the Spanish fan, with its hinge in the Caribbean, had spread from Florida to California, from Cumaná, Venezuela, in the south, to the Strait of Juan de Fuca, between Vancouver Island and northwestern Washington, in the north.

. . .   *Absorption by Conquest*

The first Spanish Americans to come to the United States were not immigrants at all but were acquired people taken over by the territorial acquisitions of the United States. It is a long story—and in the main a shameful one—that began when the United States, seeking ports on the Gulf of Mexico, annexed West Florida in 1810. It ended with the Gadsden Purchase in 1853. In the intervening forty-three years the United States by purchase, by annexation, but primarily by military conquest acquired from Spain and Mexico the whole of what is now Florida, Texas, New Mexico, Arizona, California, Nevada, Utah, and parts of what are now Colorado, Kansas, Oklahoma, and Wyoming. Until the time of this conquest the history of Texas, New Mexico, Arizona, and California was the history of Mexico. At the close of the war against Mexico the United States acquired through the Guadalupe-Hidalgo Treaty, in 1848, a

---

[5] McHenry, *op. cit.*, p. 77.

territory that was more than half of Mexico and larger than France and Germany combined. The Mexicans, who were sparsely scattered throughout this huge land mass, did not come to the United States; the United States came to them. They and their ancestors had been living on this land for roughly 250 years. They were products of Spanish colonization, and therefore a mixture of Spanish and Indian stock. Until the English-speaking world interrupted their insular seclusion they experienced little change in their personal lives or in their village-centered community. These Spanish Americans who were annexed by conquest were neither trespassers nor immigrants. By virtue of nearly three hundred years' occupation of the land they were an indigenous people.

The Mexican and Spanish colonials gained by territorial acquisition were largely mestizos and their descendants remain so. In the last century there has been little intermarriage between Hispanos and other mestizos. The Hispanos have held aloof from Indians and Mexicans from south of the border. Their feeling of superiority to lately immigrated Mexicans is a source of tension and conflict that prevents close cooperation and a common community life among these two Spanish American groups.

. . .   *The Modern Influx*

Since the boundary between Mexico and the United States after the war was arbitrary and geographically unnatural, there was nothing to interrupt the Mexicans' customary free movement north and south. The Rio Grande was in effect a bridge rather than a barrier; the desert was passable; the invisible, unmarked line of political division was no hindrance. So the Mexicans did after the war what they had done before; they moved north and returned south at will. In fact, the migration increased after 1850. Political and economic instability in Mexico and a parallel need for cheap labor in the United States stimulated the northward

migration of Mexicans. There was at that time little effort
on either side of the border to restrict this illegal flow of
population from one country to another. The Mexican Government was preoccupied with its own domestic problems;
the United States demanded a fresh source of cheap labor
to take care of the needs of its rapidly expanding economy.

This emigration of Mexicans to the United States reached
crest stage in the twenty-year period from 1909 to 1929, a
score of the stormiest years in Mexican history and the most
prosperous in the history of the United States. Carey Mc-
Williams estimates that from 1900 to 1930 "nearly ten per
cent of the total population of Mexico" [6]—roughly a million
people—entered the United States. Most of these immigrants
settled along the border. In addition, a large but indeter-
minable number of illegal entries—"wetbacks"—have crossed
the border into the United States. In 1951, officials of the
United States and Mexico reached an agreement for the
seasonal entrance into the United States of *braceros,* contract laborers who would come for a few months of work and
then return home. The purpose of the United States in in-
augurating this program was to stop what had become
virtually an invasion of cheap labor, disadvantaging American workmen. The Mexican Government sought, through
contract, to insure that their nationals would receive fair
wages. Some of the *braceros* settled in the United States
and became citizens. In recent years tighter border controls
by the United States and Mexican Governments have restricted, but certainly not eliminated, the entry of "wetbacks." There have also been periodic efforts in the United
States to limit the number of *braceros* who entered the
country legally. The purpose of this effort has been to protect the American worker. In May, 1963, the United States

---

* McWilliams, *op. cit.,* p. 163.

House of Representatives voted to end the *bracero* program at the end of the year but later the Senate reopened the matter and extended the program.

Most of the Mexican immigrants who crossed the border into this country in great mass during the past century came from the central Mexico states of Michoacán, Jalisco, and Guanajuato, states that are still rural and in which the majority of people live in villages of less than 2,500 people and are engaged in agriculture. These immigrants belonged, in the main, to the class of landless peons and were mestizos, with the Indian strain predominating. They brought with them their own problems of superstition, poverty, disease, and ignorance. They met problems of rejection, indifference, neglect, and exploitation—all of which challenge us as we consider the responsibility of the Protestant churches to the Spanish Americans in their midst.

It is sometimes humorously remarked that the first Puerto Rican immigrant to the continental United States was the first governor of Puerto Rico, Juan Ponce de León, the discoverer of Florida. But to speak today of Puerto Ricans as immigrants is to confuse terms. They, too, like the Mexicans north of the Rio Grande and the 32° parallel, entered the United States as a spoil of war, the Puerto Ricans as a result of the defeat of Spain by the United States in 1898. For nineteen years Puerto Rico was a United States colony. Its people, annexed by conquest, became citizens of this country when Congress passed the Jones Act in 1917. Therefore, when Puerto Ricans go to Miami, Chicago, or New York City, they are no more immigrants than are Iowans who go to California. However, when the Puerto Rican comes to the continental United States he has many of the characteristics of an alien immigrant. Though he may speak English, his first language is Spanish; whether he is light or dark, he is racially distinguishable; though he is an American citizen, his traditions and customs have a Spanish flavor.

When he moves from the island to the continent he becomes a stranger in his own nation.

The Puerto Rican migration to the continent is unique
in other respects. As an American citizen, the Puerto Rican
needs no passport when he travels to the United States. His
migration is by air, the first such influx in American history.
He can fly from San Juan to New York City, to Chicago,
or to Miami nonstop in a few hours, and he can return with
equal speed and ease. Air travel has made it possible for the
Puerto Rican to be a commuting migrant and is one explanation—there are others—of the fact that Puerto Ricans tend
to settle near the port of entry rather than spread into other
areas of the United States.

The migration from Puerto Rico to the United States began
before 1898. The 1910 census found Puerto Ricans living in
39 states. But the migration did not reach significant annual
proportions until the close of World War II. According to
the U. S. Immigration and Naturalization Service in San
Juan, the net migration of Puerto Ricans to the mainland,
in round numbers, was as follows: in 1945, 13,000; in 1946,
40,000; in 1956, 52,000; in 1959, 30,000. The peak year occurred in 1953, when 69,124 came from the island to the
United States. It is believed that the migration will now level
off for a few years at around 10,800, the figure for 1962. Since
many Puerto Ricans travel back and forth and since some
do so several times a year, exact statistics are difficult to
obtain.

Why do Puerto Ricans come to the mainland? There is
no one answer to this question. Undoubtedly, a primary
motivation is the desire of Puerto Ricans, like Mexicans, to
improve their standard of living. Population density for
Puerto Rico's somewhat more than two and a quarter million people is 687 persons per square mile. Despite the fabu-
lous progress of the island's economy under Governor Luis
Muñoz Marín's "Operation Bootstrap" program, Puerto Rico

is still, in the Governor's words, "a land of flattering statistics and distressing realities." The island's improving economy is still not able to absorb the rapidly increasing population; the people migrate in search of a better life. Note, a *better* life. A Columbia University study by Dr. Elena Padilla, a Puerto Rican anthropologist, showed that 85 per cent of the Puerto Ricans coming to the United States left jobs there to do so. But the per capita income, even though rising rapidly —it reached $621 in 1961—is far less than that in the United States.

In explaining the migration, some studies stress the fact that the United States national income and Puerto Rican migration rise and fall together. For example, in 1954, the migration dropped 69 per cent, following the "rolling recession" in 1953. The 1957 recession also caused a drop, and in 1961, several factors affecting the labor market caused a net outflow from the United States of minus 1,754 Puerto Ricans. The indication is that Puerto Ricans, like Mexicans, come to the United States when they are needed and do not come when they are not needed. We can conclude that they do not come, as their critics claim, to go on relief; they come to work and to find through that work a better standard of living for themselves and their children. They come because there is a job waiting for them. Through what Clarence Senior, professor at Columbia University and consultant to the secretary of labor of the Commonwealth of Puerto Rico, calls "the family intelligence network," reports on the labor market flow between mainland and island. These reports, based on job and other opportunities, regulate the traffic between Puerto Rico and mainland airports.

The latest wave of Spanish-speaking immigrants has since 1959 brought approximately 170,000 Cuban refugees to Greater Miami, Florida. Even United States Government agencies have no exact statistics. These latest immigrants are escapees fleeing from the Castro government. Despite the

restrictions imposed on travel by the Cuban Government,
the elimination of flights from Havana to Miami, the dangers
of traveling the ninety miles of open sea in small boats, the
exodus continues. Through 1962—the peak year for Cuban
immigration to the United States—the Cuban refugees
entered Florida at the rate of more than six thousand a
month. This current Cuban immigration is turbulent and
unpredictable. Most of these refugees hope and expect to
return to Cuba. When that will happen, how many more
Cubans will come to the United States, to what extent and
at what rate the refugees will radiate from the Miami area to
other parts of the United States, how many of the refugees
will give up the hope of returning to Cuba and seek citizenship in the United States—these possibilities are presently
unpredictable.

These are the principal Spanish American groups in the
United States: Mexican Americans, the descendants of
Spanish colonials (Hispanos), Puerto Ricans, and Cubans.
In addition, there is a small number of Americans who came,
or whose ancestors came, from other parts of the Caribbean,
from Central America, and from South America. Included in
this group are a number of students from Spanish-speaking
countries. They are resident in the United States for only a
few years, but their presence here is an opportunity of great
importance to the Protestant witness. The number of recent
immigrants from Spain is very small.

.   .   .   *Identities and Diversities*

It is important to remember that the phrase "Spanish American" is a general, loose classification that includes
a great variety of people. It is, let us note first, a legitimate
and useful classification. This designation may someday lose
its usefulness and disappear in the American melting pot,
as have others. But that day is far off. Until it arrives there
is value in a classification that identifies a people who share

a common mother tongue—even though some of them no longer speak or read it fluently—who in varying degrees were touched by a culture that radiated from Spain four and a half centuries ago, who are distinguishable from Anglo-Americans in physical and cultural traits, who sense and experience a group solidarity, and who think of themselves as Spanish Americans.

But this classification, though useful, is also dangerous. It tempts us to stereotype Spanish Americans, to lump them together as though there were no distinguishing differences between various subgroups. Despite the broad identities there are significant diversities. The differences between the national groups—Mexican Americans, Puerto Ricans, Cubans, and Hispanos—are obvious. Lyle Saunders stresses the fact that there are diversities within these groups as well. Writing of the Spanish Americans of the Southwest, for example, he says:

The Spanish-speaking group is not an easy one to delimit or define. The group is not homogeneous, as is popularly supposed, but is made up of persons with a wide range of physical and cultural characteristics. Many have blond or red hair, blue eyes, and fair skin. Many are quite dark, with black hair and black or brown eyes. Most are somewhere between these extremes. Some of them belong to families that have been in the Southwest two hundred years or more; some of them crossed the border from Mexico just yesterday. Some are unskilled, migrant workers, owning nothing, living in the deepest poverty. Some are highly trained technicians and professionals whose homes are indistinguishable from those of their Anglo colleagues and fellow workers. Some speak only Spanish; some know no Spanish and speak only English.[7]

We might add that through intermarriage some of them now have English, French, and Irish surnames.

---

[7] Saunders, Lyle. *The Spanish-Speaking Population of Texas*, p. 7. Austin: The University of Texas Press, 1949.

Spanish Americans are, then, next to Negroes, the second largest distinguishable minority in the United States. They are not a homogeneous people, but there are grounds on which they can be classified as an ethnic enclave within American society. They have a strong "we" sense. This sense of identity comes not only from cultural cohesives internal to the group but also from external Anglo-American pressures. In fact, Carey McWilliams considers these external pressures an important factor in the Spanish Americans' sense of group identity: ". . . the sense of cleavage from or opposition to the Anglos has always been an important factor in their lives and it is this feeling which gives cohesion to the group." [8]

· · ·   *Nomenclature*

It has proved impossible to bring all the diverse elements of Spanish American society in the continental United States together under one name acceptable to all of them, and this difficulty is compounded by the fact that Spanish Americans are naturally sensitive to and easily offended by the names Anglo-Americans give them. For example, George I. Sánchez, director of the Center for International Education, University of Texas, and an authority on Spanish Americans, once said, "My people in New Mexico—I am originally a New Mexican—prefer to be called Spanish Americans. They'll fight, if you call them Mexicans." But American citizens who came to Texas from Mexico and their descendants also resent being called Mexicans and are in courtesy given the soft, inaccurate, and meaningless title, "Latin Americans." There are more than a dozen proper names applied to Spanish Americans in the United States with no intended offense.

In this study we are arbitrarily using the collective title "Spanish American." It is an inadequate term because it

---

[8] McWilliams, *op. cit.*, p. 8.

tends to subordinate the predominant Indian strain and, as Dr. Sánchez says, gathers too many people under one umbrella. Too, it is sometimes resented as implying a partial acceptance in the general American society. But such terms as "Spanish-speaking Americans," "Americans of Spanish surnames," "Hispano Americans" are awkward and even more inadequate. It is best for the churches in their ministry to these people to defer to local customs and avoid offending local sensitivities. But for an inclusive term, "Spanish Americans" is preferable. The noun in this term—"Americans"— is friendly and inclusive; the adjective—"Spanish"—gives to the noun a proper, generally acceptable, inoffensive, ethnic definition. In dealing with special geographic divisions and in identifying particular groups, we must use more specific titles. Even though many of the Cubans, some of the Mexicans, and most of the visiting, Spanish-speaking students in the United States are not citizens, our inclusive term "Spanish Americans" embraces them and keeps them in focus as a concern of the Protestant churches.

⊰ 2   WHERE THEY LIVE AND WHAT THEY DO

                                Numbers and Places

. . .   By the middle years of the twentieth century there were approximately 5,500,000 Spanish Americans in the United States and by far the greater part of them were native born rather than immigrants. We are reduced, however, to an educated guess in this enumeration. The 1960 United States Census of population gave us little aid in estimating the number of Spanish Americans in the continental United States. It enumerated the foreign born by their mother tongue and the foreign stock—first and second generation citizens—according to their country of origin. But most Spanish Americans in the continental United States are not in these terms foreign born or of foreign stock. Their ancestors have lived in what is now the United States for many more than two generations.

For our purposes broad estimates will serve. In round numbers we are assuming the following numbers and distributions of Spanish Americans: in Texas, 1,500,000; in California, 1,400,000; in metropolitan New York, 900,000; in New Mexico, 380,000; in Florida, 270,000; in Arizona, 260,000; distributed throughout various regions of the continental United States, 700,000. The difficulty in securing an accurate account is also due to the drifting of Spanish Americans into the mainstream of American life. This drift robs us of statistics but is evidence of the beginning of a wholesome integration of Spanish Americans with the general life in the United States.

The circumstances creating congested and isolated settlements of Spanish Americans vary slightly from place to place, but two of these conditions are general. Having traveled from one country to another, most immigrants do not have the money and sometimes not the will to move inland at once. Second, most immigrants settle where they have relatives or friends who create for them a somewhat hospitable community. Most newcomers to the United States have been greeted by a hostile resident population that has ostracized them and forced them into ghettos. Despite Emma Lazarus' beckoning words on the Statue of Liberty, the people of the United States have not always been hospitable to the ". . . tired, . . . poor, . . . huddled masses" that have come through its golden door. Irish, Italian, Polish, Chinese, Japanese, Puerto Ricans, and Cubans have in turn been rejected, crowded into slums, exploited, isolated, and forced to remain strangers in their adopted land.

There are, of course, other circumstances that have pinned Spanish Americans to the fringes of this country. When Mexican territory was seized by the United States in the Mexican War, the people who lived in that territory remained where they were. Without moving at all they were transferred from one country to another merely by the signing of a series of treaties. In time these people were joined by Mexican immigrants who, entering the United States, settled close to the border. The terrain and climate were identical with that of the land they left. The prevailing language and customs were familiar. The inland was unknown and hostile. Consequently there developed a heavy concentration of Spanish Americans all along the two thousand mile border between Mexico and the United States. The reluctance of these people to move inland, their high birth rate, and a continuing immigration developed along this border many communities in which Spanish Americans outnumbered all other ethnic groups.

As the chief link between Mexico and the United States and as the northern part of one thousand miles of the border, Texas soon acquired through immigration and natural increase more Spanish Americans than any other state. We estimate more than 1,500,000 Spanish Americans in Texas, nearly one-sixth of the total population of the state. The nearer the border the higher the percentage, with some counties being more than 75 per cent Spanish American. Too, through this region come most of the "wetbacks," hundreds of thousands of them. The nature of their entry and their skill in escaping controls and censuses make an accurate numbering impossible. Here, too, are the ports of entry through which came the *braceros*, who from 1951 to 1963 entered the country legally on work permits. Both of these groups have used the Lower Rio Grande Valley as the hub from which they have radiated through Texas and to the north as migrant labor and as the base to which they have returned, thus adding to the Spanish American congestion in the southern and western borderlands of Texas. In her study of this development, Pauline R. Kibbe said, "The United States-Mexico border is the most extensive geographical area in which two of the principal cultures of this hemisphere actually meet. More than half of that border, approximately one thousand miles, is also the southern boundary of Texas." [1]

Similar circumstances have also concentrated Spanish Americans in New Mexico—40 per cent of the state's population; in Arizona—20 per cent of the people; in California—six-sevenths of them in the metropolitan areas of 17 of California's 58 counties. There has been a massive migration of Spanish Americans away from the border to Colorado, where the need for "stoop labor" has drawn 100,000 Mexican Americans. Altogether, nearly four million Spanish Americans live in the broad, irregular band that sweeps from San Francisco in the northwest to Brownsville, Texas, in the southeast. Except for the migrant laborers and their seasonal excursions, the Spanish Americans of the Southwest have been slow to move in great numbers into other parts of the United States. There is a substantial concentration of Mexican Americans in metropolitan Chicago, Detroit, and Kansas City, Missouri, but no similar resettlement outside of the Southwest.

Whether Spanish Americans of this region spread out over the United States in the next generation will depend on several factors, not the least of which is the reception given the venturesome few who try their luck in other parts of the country. But the flow of Spanish Americans from the Southwest will depend also on two closely related developments: continuing immigration and the possibility of increased problems of overcrowding and unemployment; and,

---

[1] Kibbe, Pauline R. *Latin Americans in Texas*, p. 29. Albuquerque: The University of New Mexico Press, 1946.

on the other hand, the contrary factor—the speed and thoroughness of the integration of the Spanish American in the cultural, political, and economic life of the booming Southwest. If the integration succeeds, Spanish Americans will stay put; if it fails, there will be an exodus of Spanish Americans from the Southwest similar to the flight of Mexicans from Mexico.

Since immigrants tend to settle near the port of entry and since many Puerto Ricans have no intention of breaking their ties with the island, the bulk of the Puerto Ricans in the continental United States are in New York City and adjacent areas. According to reports available from the Commonwealth of Puerto Rico's Migration Division, Department of Labor, located in New York City, there are about 900,000 Puerto Ricans in the United States. (This figure excludes data for Puerto Ricans in Arizona, California, Colorado, New Mexico, and Texas, which list persons with Hispanic surnames.) About 700,000 Puerto Ricans live in New York City: 36.8 per cent in Manhattan; 30.5 per cent in the Bronx; 29.4 per cent in Brooklyn; 2.9 per cent in Queens; and 0.4 per cent in Richmond.

As the Puerto Rican population rises in metropolitan New York, these newcomers flow in increasing numbers into the adjacent states of New Jersey and Connecticut. New Jersey, the second largest state in the number of Puerto Ricans, has roughly about 45,000: Jersey City area, 15,000; Newark, 13,000; Paterson, Clifton, and Passaic, 9,000; Middlesex County (which includes Perth Amboy), 5,000; Trenton, 2,000; Atlantic City, 900; the remainder scattered in smaller communities. Connecticut, as a part of the New York City metropolitan complex, has about 13,000 Puerto Ricans: 6,000 in Bridgeport; 3,000 in Hartford; 1,000 in New Haven; 1,000 in Waterbury; and others in New Britain, Norwalk, and Stamford. Illinois is third, with 35,000 in Chicago and environs. Direct, relatively inexpensive, nonstop flights from

San Juan to Chicago explain the size of the colony of Puerto Ricans in the Chicago area. As a port of entry Chicago is little less convenient than New York City. That fact, coupled with the high level of employment in metropolitan Chicago, accounts for the fact that a significant number of Puerto Ricans now enter the United States through O'Hare International Airport. Pennsylvania figures list 26,000 Puerto Ricans, with 22,000 in the Philadelphia area and about 1,600 in the Allentown-Bethlehem-Easton area. Florida has 14,000, with almost 12,000 in the Miami area. There are also notable settlements in Cleveland, Youngstown, and Warren, Ohio; in Gary, Hammond, and East Chicago, Indiana; Washington, D.C.; Buffalo and Rochester, New York; Milwaukee, Wisconsin; and Detroit, Michigan.

The proportion of Puerto Ricans settling in New York has been declining steadily. Indications are that the percentage is leveling off at about 60, and there are wholesome signs that the group will spread over the United States more rapidly than any ethnic group that has entered this country in the past. Under favorable circumstances—which the churches must help create—the clusters of Puerto Ricans outside New York City will draw to them an increasing number of Puerto Ricans. It is predicted that by 1975, there will be more than a million Puerto Ricans in New York City. This is probable, but it is also a possibility that an increasing number of Puerto Ricans will flow into other parts of the United States.

There have been Spanish-speaking people in Florida since the peninsula and parts of the gulf coast were settled by the Spanish in the sixteenth century. When the Cuban refugees began fleeing from the Fidel Castro government to the Florida mainland, there was already a Spanish-speaking community of 100,000 people in Miami and a smaller but significant one in Tampa, consisting mostly of immigrants from or descendants of immigrants from Cuba. Since the flight

from Cuba began in 1959, roughly 170,000 additional Cubans
have come to Florida, the great majority coming directly to
or making their way more gradually to Greater Miami (Dade
County). Unfortunately for them and for the city, these
escapees arrived in Miami at a time when it was suffering
severe economic distress. Without heavy industry and with
more than thirty thousand unemployed local residents,
Greater Miami has not been able to absorb the influx of
Cubans. The Cuban congestion in Dade County, compound-
ing the economic and social distress, has been relieved by
the relocation of approximately sixty thousand Cuban refugees in other parts of the United States. But the Cuban
refugee, having pulled up his roots once, is reluctant to do
so again. He prefers Miami because of its large Spanish-
speaking population and because he still hopes that an early
collapse of the present Cuban Government will enable him
to return home. Moreover, inadequate as it is, the welfare
aid received by the refugee in Florida may have to be for-
feited if he moves elsewhere.

Every Cuban refugee who comes to Greater Miami comes
under the care and direction of the United States Department of Health, Education, and Welfare. He is registered
and interviewed and his name, family status, vocational experience, reasons for leaving Cuba, financial resources, etc.,
are permanently recorded. He can qualify for registration and
receive an identification card if he left Cuba after January 1,
1959, if he is located in Miami, and if he has passed through
the Cuban Refugee Center provided by the Department of
Health, Education, and Welfare. From the Dade County
Public Health Department the Cuban refugee receives
X-rays, inoculations, and medical examinations. He is then
referred to whichever private agency he chooses: Catholic
Relief Services, Church World Service, United Hebrew Immigrant Aid Society, or the International Rescue Committee.
Following this referral and preliminary interviews by the

private agency, the refugee goes to Florida State Public Assistance, where social workers determine his need and the amount of welfare help he can receive. Since the public assistance program provides a maximum aid of $100 a month whatever the size of the family, and since most of the refugees pay $60 or $70 a month for rent, the plight of the unemployed Cuban refugee is a serious one.

.   .   .   *Trends*

Spanish Americans are the largest ethnic group in the United States with a language other than English as the mother tongue. They are—with the exception of the Indian Americans—the only such ethnic group that is increasing rather than declining in numbers. The high birth rate of Spanish American residents, the quota-free immigration of Western Hemisphere peoples, the freedom of Puerto Ricans and Cuban refugees to enter this country at will, and the slowness of the integrating process guarantee a steady rise in the Spanish American population of the United States. Ten years ago it could be said with some confidence that "the Spanish-language press is on the decline and the English-language press for Mexicans is on the increase; it is probable that in 15 years the Spanish-language press will virtually have died out." [2] Today that statement can be made with the same confidence about Mexican Americans, but certainly the influx of Puerto Ricans makes the prophecy of the end of the Spanish-language press in the United States premature. *La Prensa* and *El Diario*, both daily, Spanish-language papers published in New York and purchasable at some newsstands in Chicago, have an increasing number of subscribers. It is estimated that over half the Puerto Ricans in New York City read a Spanish-language daily newspaper, that 84 per cent speak Spanish at least in their homes, and

---

[2] Burma, John H. *Spanish-Speaking Groups in the United States*, p. 99. Durham: Duke University Press, 1954.

that nearly as large a number prefer Spanish on the radio. Spanish Americans in the United States are and will remain a bilingual people for many years to come, at least as long as they are isolated from the mainstream of American life.

Spanish Americans are a younger people than the Anglo-Americans of the same regions in which they live. The percentage of persons under twenty years of age among Spanish Americans is 48.8 per cent; the corresponding percentage among Anglo-Americans is 32 per cent. This factor alone will produce a booming Spanish American population in the next generation. Add the fact that an average of fifty thousand Mexicans now enter the United States as immigrants each year and it is obvious that an immense mission field for the Protestant churches grows up in their midst.

Another population trend worth noting is the gravitation of Spanish Americans toward urban centers. Already a majority of the Spanish-speaking people in the United States live in cities rather than rural areas, and the direction of their population shift is toward increasing urbanization. This flow of Spanish Americans toward cities and toward the great metropolitan complexes is characteristic of our whole society, but it is well to discard the popular notion that Spanish Americans are a rural people. Even the migrant workers tend to retreat in the off-season periods from a rural to a city life. Urbanization requires of the Spanish Americans—as it does of other Americans oriented to village and rural life—difficult psychological and sociological adjustments. For the migrants this problem is particularly acute. The strong folk-sense characteristic of Mexican American life in the past is shattered by depersonalizing city life, and there are resultant psychological and sociological problems. It is still too early to know how speedily and well Spanish Americans will master these problems. Studies of the effects of urbanization upon Spanish American life are thus far inadequate; even statistical data are unreliable.

. . .   *Jobs*

To write briefly of the work done by Spanish Americans in the United States requires the use of general terms. Unfortunately, this can be done with a fair degree of accuracy. Throughout the Southwest there are "Mexican jobs," just as there are "Negro jobs" throughout the South. There are exceptions, of course, and those exceptions gradually increase; but in the main, Spanish Americans in the Southwest are offered only low status employment. When Oriental immigration was barred by law and European immigration was put on a quota basis, the need for cheap labor for agriculture and the railroads lured Mexicans across the border. They and their children were caught in a caste system from which, without proper education and leadership, they could not escape. What the social psychologists call the "self-fulfilling prophecy" operates in the lives of Spanish Americans as well as Negroes. Pinned by circumstance to "stoop labor," low wages, part-time employment, and job classification fixed by the powerful ethnic majority, Spanish Americans are poor, have a high rate of disease, and receive second-rate education. Their poverty, disease, and ignorance are then used by the majority as "proof" that Spanish Americans are incapable of rising in the world and deserve only "Mexican jobs." When they move in search of a better life they take whatever jobs they can get, usually at the lowest menial level.

Despite the improving job situation in the Southwest, most Spanish Americans in that region are still unskilled laborers and the large majority are engaged in agriculture. Even when Mexican Americans in the Southwest rise above the "stoop labor" level, they still receive differential treatment in wages, tenure, and promotion. Spanish American lawyers, doctors, nurses, teachers, businessmen are, of course, much more fortunate than the laborers; nevertheless, they, too, experience the discrimination suffered by their minority.

In the Chicago area, as in the Southwest, some Mexican Americans have moved into semiskilled categories. But most of the Mexican Americans in Chicago are hired at the unskilled level in steel mills, meat-packing plants, and on railroads.

Like the Mexicans, the Puerto Ricans have suffered the fate of all immigrants who have come in waves to meet this nation's labor demands: the lowest-paying jobs, the worst and simultaneously most expensive housing, overcrowded schools, prejudice, and social rejection. In addition, roughly one-fifth of the Puerto Rican immigrants meet a more open and flagrant color barrier in the United States than they experienced in Puerto Rico.

A large number of Puerto Ricans are absorbed by New York City's clothing industry, its hotels and restaurants, and in hundreds of light industries where their manual dexterity is an asset. There are also some Puerto Rican doctors, ministers, lawyers, policemen, social workers, teachers, and independent businessmen. Puerto Ricans in New York City also own and operate several thousand small establishments, such as barber shops, grocery stores, pharmacies, laundries. Beyond the periphery of New York City many Puerto Ricans are employed, often on a part-time basis, by the truck farms in New Jersey.

We have noted that Dade County (Miami), Florida, has not been able to absorb the recent influx of Cubans into its economy despite the willingness of most Cubans to take whatever jobs are available. Stories of formerly wealthy and professional Cubans working now at menial tasks are numerous and many of these stories are true. The employment problem for Cubans in Florida remains serious.

The need to write in particular of the jobs of Spanish Americans is in itself evidence that employment on all levels is not completely open to persons of this group on the basis of their ability.

The 1960 report to the President on domestic migratory farm labor stated:

Each year approximately 500,000 of these workers leave their homes and travel throughout the country to work on American farms. Very often their lives are characterized by lack of adequate employment, low wages, poor housing, lack of education, lack of health and welfare services, and in some cases, unsafe vehicles for transportation. . . . Who are the migrants? They are chiefly families from the South and Southwest—Negroes, Mexican-Americans, "Anglos," and American Indians—who follow the harvests for thousands of miles each year to avoid either unemployment or low wages at home. . . . For performing this vital job, the migrant earns an average of about $900 per year and lives a life that is characterized by "exclusion." . . . It is the children of migrants who are more drastically affected by this nomadic way of life. Not only do these children suffer from the disadvantages that handicap the whole migrant community— health hazards, inadequate food and housing, lack of stable family life, lack of opportunity to belong to and participate in community living which makes for responsible citizenship—but their whole future can be adversely affected by two additional aspects of the migrant situation: Because of the low earnings of their parents, migrant children are very often found working in the fields, sometimes illegally, in order that the family income may be sufficient to pay bills. Secondly, because of their constant mobility, migrant children are deprived of the opportunity to obtain the kind of education that would enable them to make their own lives an improvement over those of their parents.[3]

How many of these migrants are Spanish Americans? Exact figures are not available, but all indications are that the great majority of the migrant laborers and their families are

[3] *Second Report of the President's Committee on Domestic Migratory Farm Labor*, pp. 3, 4, 5. United States Department of Labor, 1960.

Spanish American. In 1961, 300,000 *braceros*—sometimes called Nationals—entered the United States from Mexico for seasonal work. This figure was 100,000 less than the average number of *braceros* from 1956 through 1959. The establishment of a minimum wage scale for Nationals in California, Michigan, Wisconsin, Colorado, Texas, and Arkansas —low as the minimum is—reduced the demand for Nationals and simultaneously and consequently increased the number of immigrants seeking citizenship from 23,000 in 1959 to more than 50,000 in 1962. This decrease in the need for Nationals is a decisive factor in the increasing hope to bring the *bracero* program to an end. However, when we add the total number of Spanish American immigrants who have already established citizenship, the "wetbacks" who still evade border guards, the Spanish American migrants from the Southwest, and the Puerto Rican migrant farmers in the Middle Atlantic states, it appears that Spanish Americans make up the bulk of America's migrant labor force.

Spanish American migrant labor is concentrated in the border states, particularly in the cotton fields of Texas and in the fruit and vegetable farms of California. The laborers are employed heavily in the beet fields of Colorado, Montana, Nebraska, and Kansas. They harvest fruit and vegetables in Michigan, Wisconsin, Minnesota, Washington, Louisiana, and Arkansas. In 1960, 10,770 Spanish Americans in 867 units, most of them from Texas, worked cherries, cucumbers, peas, sugar beets, sweet corn, and other vegetables in Wisconsin. The Michigan Migrant Ministry, an arm of the Michigan Council of Churches, reported in 1962 a total of 78,730 migrant laborers. Of these, 12,730 were male Mexican Nationals, 200 were from the British West Indies, and the remainder were Spanish Americans, Anglo-Americans, and Negroes. The spread of Spanish American migrant laborers to states far from the Mexican border is illustrated in these two states.

The migrant laborer is the low man on the economic and social totem pole. He receives the lowest annual wage of any American laborer and is excluded from almost all state and Federal social laws, such as workmen's compensation, unemployment insurance, and health and welfare services. The Spanish American migrant is by necessity forced into a way of life that is repugnant to him. His natural gregariousness and his folk-life and village traditions make him prefer a settled rather than a nomadic life. He is underpaid, poorly housed, inadequately fed, highly vulnerable to disease, and deprived of realistic hope that his children will fare better than he does. His transportation from job to job is uncertain, uncomfortable, and hazardous. (Many migrant workers have been killed while riding in unsafe buses and trucks.) And in this oppressed society the migrant—sometimes illiterate and therefore ignorant of such American labor standards as do give him a modicum of protection—is largely defenseless before the exploiter. All of this is particularly true for the large numbers of Mexican Nationals who work in the United States as cotton pickers. As a report from the National Council of the Protestant Episcopal Church put it: "There is no past for these Mexican migrants and there seems to be little future."

· · ·   Homes

For many Spanish Americans in the Southwest, home is a shack in the slums or an adobe hut in the village. Despite slum clearance programs since the war and the removal of some Spanish Americans to better neighborhoods, the slums remain. Spanish Americans in Texas report that there has been great progress in their state in the moving of their people to good residential areas of the larger cities and in their participation in government. Nevertheless, the plight of the people who cannot for one reason or another move to a better neighborhood remains critical.

Like all such depressed urban areas the so-called "Little Mexicos" or "Mexican colonies" are pools of squalor, congestion, and disease. Swallowed up and sealed off in the big cities or cut off and isolated by railroad tracks, a river, a highway in the smaller cities and towns, these slums are the breeding places of disease and despair. Slums are both victims and villains. They are products of the poverty and despair of those who live there and of the indifference and neglect of those who do not live there. In turn, the slum becomes the villain, producing an ignorant, diseased, beaten people. When the slum dweller accumulates enough money to move elsewhere, he often finds his way barred by neighborhoods closed to members of his group. Most Spanish Americans in the Southwest are still caught in this trap.

The lot of Spanish Americans in New York City and other metropolitan areas in the North and Northeast is no better. For the Puerto Rican in New York City, home is frequently one or two rooms with a shared bath in Spanish Harlem. For this space, into which he may have to crowd a large family, he pays twenty dollars or more a week for each room. There has been little improvement, if any, in the condition of Puerto Rican housing in New York City as described in 1953: "New York's Puerto Rican sections in 1953 probably ranked among the worst in the world. This was not because of the age or the exteriors of the buildings but because of the number of people crowded into small spaces—and because rents are so high that little is left for other needs. An American missionary described Harlem housing conditions as worse than what he had seen in China, the primary evil being the psychological collapse caused by overcrowding. It is not an overstatement." [4] Housing for Cubans in Florida, despite progress in relocation, remains substandard.

For most migrant workers, home is a dilapidated truck, a

---

[4] Abrams, Charles. *Forbidden Neighbors*, p. 60. New York: Harper & Brothers, 1955.

tattered tent, a camp shack on the edge of the field. As would be expected, the people who stand on the lowest economic rung and who move from place to place have in their housing the worst of two possible worlds—urban and rural. While there have been improvements in the housing of migrants, it remains true that they go from urban slums to rural slums and back again. In 1960, less than half the states had established and enforced housing and sanitation codes.

Hundreds of thousands of American tourists traveling in Spanish-speaking lands have heard the gracious greeting, "My house is yours." In receiving hundreds of thousands of new residents from Spanish-speaking countries, this nation has not returned the compliment. Instead, it has packed these newcomers into substandard housing in congested, unsanitary slums; made their escape difficult by restricting the better neighborhoods; and gouged from them rents greatly in excess of the true value of the housing opened to them. Urban redevelopment and the home-building boom in the nation, massive as they have been in some areas of the country, have not solved the housing needs of the two largest and most desperate minorities, Negroes and Spanish Americans.

. . .   *Projection*

Spanish Americans have been here a long time—before the Anglo-American's ancestors landed, before the nation became a nation, before the Protestant church reached this continent. They are here in great numbers, numbers that are increasing in proportions unequaled by other ethnic groups, streaming in at the rate of 50,000 a year from Mexico, 20,000 a year from Puerto Rico, and an average of 40,000 a year from Cuba. Their disease and mortality statistics are high, but their birth rate would be sufficient to guarantee an increasing number of Spanish Americans in the United States even though all immigration ceased.

These people have the unhappy distinction of being second only to Indians and Negroes in the marks of oppression inflicted upon them by a society that deliberately excludes them from the community, the benefits and the opportunities of a nation dominated by Anglo-Americans. And some of them—Puerto Rican and Cuban Negroes—share all the offenses heaped upon Negroes.

Two-thirds of these Americans, moreover, live in a part of the country where their nominal affiliation with the Roman Catholic Church makes them suspect to an Anglo-American population that is in that region predominantly Protestant. The ironies of history, the greed and indifference of the powerful Anglo-American majority, the neglect of all levels of government have combined to make them poorly fed, sheltered, educated, and employed. To this old, numerous, highly visible and identifiable American population, to its despair and hope, to its lack of elemental necessities, to its moral and spiritual needs, to its dormant and submerged values for other Americans, the Protestant churches are just now awakening. It is not too late to know and understand these people, to help them and be helped by them.

3   WHAT SPANISH
AMERICANS NEED

.   .   .   *Acceptance*

It may appear presumptuous for an Anglo-American to define what Spanish Americans need, but this is not necessarily so. The basic human needs are universal. The hopes and fears that everywhere attend those needs may vary from person to person, group to group; but the elemental needs are common to all men. What is required here is simply to expose those needs as they appear for Spanish

Americans under the special circumstances that characterize their personal and public lives, and to measure the wants and satisfactions of Spanish Americans against those of other ethnic groups in American society. Granted that the needs of all human beings are the same, what are the exceptional deficiencies and deprivations suffered by Spanish Americans in the United States?

The primary need, underlying and aggravating all others, is the need to be accepted. James Bryce, the British historian, regarded "a nationality as an aggregate of men drawn together and linked together by certain sentiments. The chief among these are racial sentiment and religious sentiment, but there is also that sense of community which is created by the use of a common language, the possession of a common literature, the recollection of common achievements or sufferings in the past, the existence of common customs and habits of thought, common ideals and aspirations." [1] If Bryce's definition of nationality—or any of the other classical definitions—is accepted, then we have to say of the United States that in a sense it is not a nation but an empire. It is an empire composed not of groups of nations under a single sovereign state but composed rather of groups of people under a single sovereign people. Throughout the history of this state, the sovereign group, exercising until recently almost total control over other groups, has been white, gentile, Anglo-American, and most often, but not always, Protestant. The subject and second-class peoples in this empire have been the Indian, the Negro, the Oriental, the Jew, various immigrant groups, and the Spanish American. By Bryce's definition of nationality the United States is not "one nation . . . indivisible." It is an empire in which one of the heterogeneous parts—the Spanish American—is deliberately excluded, along with the Negro and other minorities, and is

[1] Bryce, James. *International Relations*, pp. 116-117. New York: The Macmillan Co., 1922. Used by permission of Margaret V. Bryce.

burdened by the inevitable oppressions of that exclusion. This segment is rejected by another of the heterogeneous parts—the Anglo-American, who boldly acclaims his nation's oneness but who arranges for his group a society in which that oneness is withheld not only from the Negro, who is one-tenth of the nation, but also from the Spanish American, who is one-thirtieth.

Ideally, of course, the United States seeks a new kind of nationality, a pluralistic culture embracing all kinds of racial, religious, national, and cultural difference. But this is merely an ideal that in practice the dominant group has rejected. For, in fact, the dominant group is demanding nationality on Bryce's terms, a nationality of sameness rather than oneness. And this demand is particularly offensive to Americans whose race precludes sameness or who do not want to surrender cherished cultural and religious distinctions. The burden of this dilemma falls on the Spanish American as heavily as on any ethnic minority in America, including the Negro. Indeed, the Spanish American, seeking acceptance in American society, has some handicaps that the Negro does not have—a fact we merely indicate here and deal with in more detail later.

The Spanish American has none of Bryce's qualifications. He is racially distinct. Although most of these people are Caucasians and are classified as such in the United States Census, they nevertheless have the racial visibility of a special family of Caucasians. The Spanish American is nominally a Christian, and formally he usually speaks of himself as a Roman Catholic, an affiliation that does not endear him to the predominantly Protestant Anglo-Americans who meet him at the border. His first language, even though he and his forefathers may have been in this country for generations, is Spanish rather than English. His customs, literature, history, and habits of thought are not those of the great majority of American people. Moreover, like his

cousin, the Indian, he is descended from a people conquered by the United States. In theory, the American concept of nationality permits none of these distinctions to exclude the Spanish American from full citizenship. But the
notorious chasm between American principles and practices
of nationality excludes the Spanish American from full participation in the political, cultural, and economic body and
makes him, at best, a second-class citizen.

John H. Burma itemizes the discrimination that results
from this exclusion of the Spanish American:

> The prejudice and discrimination which most Mexicans meet
> in the Southwest and West is of long standing. The earliest
> impressions of Anglos in contact with Mexicans after the Mexi-
> can War annexations were that they were wretchedly poor, idle,
> and given to drinking, thieving, and gambling. These attitudes
> formed the first basis for the prejudiced stereotype of the
> Mexican which often exists today. . . . Social discrimination
> manifests itself in a variety of ways: refusing service in barber-
> shops, soda fountains, cafes, drive-ins, beauty parlors, hotels,
> bars, and recreation centers; segregation in housing, movies,
> schools, churches, and cemeteries, as well as in public buildings
> and public toilets; reluctant service in hospitals, colleges, social
> welfare offices, and courts; and even refusing to permit Mexican-
> American hostesses in USO's. Sometimes there will be signs "No
> Mexicans Allowed," "Mexicans Will Be Served in Kitchens
> Only," or "We Do Not Solicit Mexican or Negro Trade"; more
> often it is the less obtrusive but equally well understood "We
> Retain the Right to Refuse Service to Any Customer." [2]

If this seems extravagant and dated, listen to what Ralph
Estrada, former president of La Alianza Hispano-Americana, said at a conference in 1959:

> Then one might say that discrimination is pretty much a
> thing of the past in such cities as Tucson and Phoenix. One

---

[2] Burma, John H. *Spanish-Speaking Groups in the United States*,
pp. 106-108. Durham: Duke University Press, 1954.

can point to Mexican-Americans who have risen to great heights in their communities. They are admitted to the country clubs. They live in the best residential sections. They associate with high society. And yet I can point to any number of examples of a continuing discrimination in both of those communities. For instance, in Tucson it is an interesting fact that within three or four blocks of San Augustin Cathedral, which has a largely Mexican-American congregation, is another Roman Catholic church, the boundaries of which conveniently exclude virtually all the Mexican-American residential areas in that part of the city. Thus we have two churches just three or four blocks apart, one serving the Mexican-Americans and the other serving the Anglos.[3]

We have already noted the ghettoization of Puerto Ricans in New York City. We can say now that this is due not only to their gregariousness and their need for one another but also to the fact that they receive the same kind of rejection that has been received by every late-arriving immigrant group. Two facts need to be stressed. First, the problem of exclusion is particularly acute for Negro Puerto Ricans. When they meet the color bar, they are surprised, stunned, and bewildered by the extent of its exclusiveness in the continental United States. For the first time in their lives these newcomers meet institutionalized racial discrimination, something they have not known in their native Puerto Rico. Where the Puerto Rican family is itself interracial, the tensions created by racial bias and exclusion are heartbreaking and insufferable.

Second, Puerto Ricans who move outside the city meet racial and ethnic prejudice wherever they go. Middle class, educated, white Puerto Ricans sometimes make an easy adjustment to and are cordially received by the new communities and churches to which they move. But these people

---

[3] *Summary of Conference on Latin-American Relations in the Southwestern United States*, p. 18. Division of Racial Minorities, The National Council of the Protestant Episcopal Church, New York, 1959.

are few, and their experience is exceptional. The experience of the majority is liable to be like that described by Isham B. Jones in his study of Puerto Ricans in New Jersey: "The Puerto Rican, like the American Negro, is a second class citizen in his community. He is discriminated against in churches, schools, homes, places of public accommodation, and employment." [4] The Puerto Rican's feeling of strangeness in his adopted community, his search for security in the company of fellow Puerto Ricans, his difficulty with English, his physical dissimilarity to the established people in the new community, the intolerance of those people—these conditions, and others, push the incoming Puerto Ricans into the already existing patterns of exclusion and discrimination.

When the United States annexed the Southwest from Mexico, and Puerto Rico from Spain, it assumed responsibility for the people who lived there. When it receives immigrants and borrows workers from Mexico, Puerto Rico, and Cuba it has a moral and legal obligation to make available to these people all the rights and privileges promised to them—the rights of citizens and the rights of alien visitors. The nation and the people have failed that duty and, on the contrary, have humiliated and oppressed the Spanish Americans—citizens as well as aliens—by excluding them from the mainstream of American life. This exclusion is the largest single factor contributing to the debasement of the Spanish American in education, health, occupation, and general welfare. The exclusion of the Spanish American contributes in large measure to every other oppression suffered by these Americans.

The reluctance of Anglo-Americans to accept Spanish Americans and their slowness in doing so produce not only social problems for the nation but also deep psychic prob-

---

[4] Jones, Isham B. *The Puerto Rican in New Jersey: His Present Status,* p. 39. Newark: N. J. State Department of Education, Division Against Discrimination, July, 1955.

lems for the individual Spanish American. Even if he were graciously and sincerely received by the people of his new nation, he would have certain problems of "belonging" to work out. He is a man suspended between two cultures— Spanish and English—and each lures him and has a claim upon him. Ruth D. Tuck's study of a California city tells the reaction of Juan Perez to the new country: "I have exchanged the spiritual for the material. . . . I am like the man who went to the *cambiador* [the money-changer], but who could not count. I do not precisely know what I got in return. I live better, I have more things, but I do not feel at home in the world." [5] He has broken with the old but has not been accepted by the new; he has not been received but he has nothing to return to; his past and his future are blocked, and he is not at home in the present. This kind of exclusion, this alienation, can be deeply disturbing.

The Spanish American's unnerving sense of transiency is further compounded by the fact that he is caught in the transition of his people from a Spanish rural to an English urban culture. His background, or that of his immediate ancestors, is a simple, relatively slowly paced, tightly knit village life. His new environment is a complex, fast moving, impersonal urban life. So far as the rural-urban aspect of this change is concerned, the Spanish American—like the West Virginia mountaineer moving to Akron or Chicago—falls into a self-perpetuating sociological trap. It is inevitable that in the new environment he should seek security in the familiar. When he does so, he exposes himself to the partially true, but nevertheless unjustly used, charge that he is clannish, that he does not want to integrate with the community. This is obviously a rationalization for prejudice and exclusion, but it is one readily seized by those who want to use it. The Spanish American's "clannishness" is built into the

---

[5] Tuck, Ruth. *Not With the Fist*, p. 106. New York: Harcourt, Brace & World, Inc., 1946.

situation. Unless he receives a believable welcome from someone, from some group beyond his ethnic circle, he cannot break out of this trap. Security within his own group, resistance from beyond his group, drive him in upon himself. Caught in the social ghetto, the prisoner develops within himself a personal ghetto.

Is it true that the Spanish American is clannish, that he does not want to integrate with the dominant ethnic group? This is a charge that has been made against every ethnic group immigrating to the United States. It is partly true, partly false. People from the same national and cultural background do enjoy one another, seek out one another, and in a strange and hostile land need and depend upon one another. (English-speaking Americans have their colonies in Monterrey, Mexico City, Caracas.) But the emotionally charged, derogatory word "clannish" should not be used to describe this congeniality. The word has implications that are sociologically inaccurate. For the minority group set down in a strange and inhospitable land, the folk-group is a protection, a refuge. In every case in American history, the ethnic minority surrenders the security of the in-group only when it is assured that the larger society will accept members of the smaller society without prejudice and discrimination. However much it may enjoy familiar ties and find strength in its solidarity, the minority does not want the badge of inferiority, the social restraints, and the vocational and cultural limitations that are the penalties of exclusion. As it is able and is permitted to do so, the excluded minority exchanges some of the joys and protections of the similar and the familiar for a larger participation in the joys and advantages of the wider, common life.

We should not expect, nor should we encourage, the ethnic minority to abandon all of its cultural distinctions and submerge itself in the Anglo-American stream. When this happens the nation is deprived of an enriching, strengthening cross-fertilization. But we should expect, and we should encourage, the minority to identify itself with the total good of the nation, to move out of the psychic as well as the physical ghetto into the common life of the country. And we should make it possible for the minority to do this. We cannot expect a derided and deprived people to give up their so-called clannishness until those of us who belong to the socially secure majority give up our exclusiveness.

The Puerto Ricans in New York City, despite the obstacles they have encountered, are proving that an immigrating group can make a swift adjustment to its new environment despite cultural, linguistic, and racial barriers. A New York social worker, Miss Maryal Knox, said that Puerto Ricans "are being assimilated into the life of the city faster than any previous group, partly through their own impressive efforts and partly because we're learning better how to help the process." [6] The Reverend David W. Barry, executive director of the New York City Mission Society, illustrates this rapid adaptation: "No previous immigrant group so quickly numbered among its members so many policemen and welfare workers, teachers and social workers, office workers and independent businessmen, and even doctors and lawyers—after barely a dozen years in New York. And the signs of the future are in the substantial enrollment of young Puerto Ricans in the city's colleges and universities." [7] In a comment at the National Conference on Religion and Race in Chicago, January, 1963, Dr. Dan W. Dodson, professor of education, New York University, said that revivals in art in this country have frequently been produced by newly arrived ethnic groups, and that he expects New York Puerto Ricans to produce the next such revival. The coming of Puerto Ricans has, of course, created for them and for the city many

[6] Senior, Clarence. *Strangers—Then Neighbors: From Pilgrims to Puerto Ricans*, p. 32. New York: Freedom Books, 1961.

[7] *Ibid.*, p. 67.

social problems. But it is plain that in their productivity and in their creativity they have made contributions that more than balance the difficulties. And it is equally plain that they are making a resolute and successful effort to enter fully into the whole life of the city.

There is evidence also that Spanish Americans in the Southwest are ready, if encouraged, to break out of the psychological ghetto, to contribute to and identify themselves more closely with the national character. The number of Spanish Americans who participated in the armed forces in World War II—250,000 to 300,000 Spanish-speaking troops —showed their willingness, since a large per cent were volunteers, to be identified with the ordeals of our national purpose. Their service provided for a large number of Spanish Americans a broadening experience, which is being felt throughout the Spanish American community. When the sons and daughters of a people have suffered and died for their country in great numbers, it is never again quite as easy to shut that people off from the benefits and opportunities of the nation. They have acquired one of those conditions that, according to Bryce, link men in a common nationality: "common achievements or sufferings in the past."

.   .   .   *Organization*

Neither the self-awareness of the Spanish Americans nor their thus far feeble claim to total membership in the American body has been translated into effective nationwide organizations of protest and advancement. The stress belongs on the words "effective" and "nationwide," for certainly Spanish Americans have had an abundance of organizations. Indeed, the number of such fraternities is surprising when one considers the fact that the great majority of Spanish Americans come out of a recent and a remote past in which social organizations other than the family and the church were rare. John H. Burma says there were as many as seventy-two Mexican American organizations at one time in the Co-ordinating Council of Latin-American Youth in Los Angeles.[8]

Three of the larger Spanish American organizations have had a measure of success in securing fraternal and social welfare benefits for Spanish Americans. The oldest of these is the Spanish American Alliance (La Alianza Hispano-Americana). As described by Ralph Estrada,[9] it was formed in 1894 in Tucson, Arizona, by a group of businessmen as a fraternal insurance organization. The alliance has an estimated 200 to 275 lodges spread throughout the Southwest. According to Mr. Estrada, its former president, the Spanish American Alliance has three important programs seeking the advancement of the Mexican American in the Southwest. In 1955, the alliance organized its Civil Rights Department, which since that time has engaged in a number of lawsuits and other actions affecting Mexican American life: desegregating the public schools in Phoenix and Glendale, Arizona, and in El Centro, California; appearing as friend of the court in a manslaughter case prejudiced by Los Angeles newspapers; halting the abuse of Mexican Americans by sheriff's deputies in Los Angeles County; and similar activities.

Later, the alliance established the Alianza Scholarship Foundation to finance the college and university education of worthy and needy Mexican American youth. Recognizing that an uneducated youth will remain tied to the lowest level jobs, the alliance hopes to assure many capable Mexican Americans of a college education. And, third, the alliance seeks to combat communism wherever it appears in Mexico and other Central and South American countries. It proposes to do this by expanding the Alianza Internacional with lodges throughout these countries.

[8] Burma, *op. cit.*, p. 100.
[9] *Summary of Conference on Latin-American Relations, op. cit.*, pp. 20-21.

According to John H. Burma, the largest of the Spanish American organizations committed to social welfare programs is the League of United Latin-American Citizens (LULACS). This league had its beginning in Corpus Christi, Texas, in 1929 as a fusion of the Sons of America and the Sons of Texas and spread throughout the Southwest. Burma mentions another and different sort of Spanish American organization—the Mexican-American Movement. "Basically oriented toward native-born Americans of Mexican parentage, it was organized in Southern California in 1941 as an outgrowth of a yearly conference sponsored by the Los Angeles YMCA for Mexican-American young men." [10]

Notwithstanding the existence of these organizations, and many others less significant, Spanish Americans remain weak organizationally. Ralph L. Beals, professor of anthropology at U.C.L.A., says:

In general Mexican-American communities lack internal community organization to a very marked degree. Neither church, labor, fraternal, social nor political organizations exist or, if they do, they have no vitality. Only occasionally and for brief periods does effective organization develop to meet some acute crisis. The Mexican-American community lacks strikingly the middle, professional and business classes which have developed among most immigrant and ethnic groups. The contrast with the Negro group is particularly striking.[11]

One aspect of this contrast is of interest to us here. In his church—his own free, open, democratic, Protestant church —the Negro discovered his true image and began to develop his hidden capabilities. The church was for him a mirror in which, as nowhere else, he saw himself as a child of God with the dignity and potentiality of that endowment. The

[10] Burma, op. cit., p. 102.
[11] From Ralph L. Beals's 1951 address to the Fifth Annual Conference of the Southwest Council on the Education of Spanish-Speaking People, George Pepperdine College, Los Angeles, California.

church was for the Negro a laboratory in which he developed and practiced his latent skills. It was for him a social cosmos in which his people found one another and in which they pooled their sorrows and gathered their mutual strength. The church was for the Negro a voice protesting injustice and preserving his hope for a better day to come. It was a challenge, calling him to self-improvement, and under such leaders as Martin Luther King, Jr., it became an instrument that procured successes where everything else failed. Slowly paced as the rise of the Negro American has been, as far off as his goal may still be, without the church, which served him as school, fortress, and frontier, the cultural lag that slavery imposed on the Negro might not have been overcome for centuries.

We shall examine this deficiency in Spanish American life more closely later. For the moment, we can say that Spanish Americans—who should be described as predominantly non-Protestant, since most of them cannot be factually described as Roman Catholic—have lacked that particular social, democratizing, and civilizing instrument that has been the greatest help to the Negro in his self-fulfillment —the Protestant church. We can safely assume that the history of Spanish-speaking people in the United States would have been vastly different from what it has been if they could have had, as the Negro did, the creative, liberating experience of a Protestant church governed by the people.

·   ·   ·   *Leadership*

Students of Spanish American life in the United States are in general agreement that this ethnic community has been deficient in leadership. Carey McWilliams, whose studies are sound, and who certainly could not be accused of bias, made this point in his address to the Protestant Episcopal Conference on Latin-American Relations in the Southwestern United States: "One of the major difficulties with

Latin-American relations in the Southwest is that the Spanish-speaking people have lacked spokesmen. I am speaking, of course, in long retrospect. What has been lacking, in part, is the direct expression of the people themselves." [12] Others have made a similar and equally categorical appraisal.

This is a peculiar and amazing phenomenon. The rise of the strong man who speaks for, or who, in some cases, merely pretends to speak for, the people is a characteristic development in Spanish-speaking countries. In fact, this characteristic has a Spanish name—*caudillismo* or *caudillaje* —that means either responsible leadership or tyranny. The homelands of Spanish Americans have had strong, responsible leaders: Mexico, its Juárez; Cuba, its José Martí; Puerto Rico, its Muñoz Marín. But the Americans who came to the United States from these countries have not yet produced a comparable leadership in art, literature, or politics. The absence of such leadership at this, and at a lower, level has been a serious social and political handicap in the Spanish American struggle for an equitable share in the national life.

There are signs that encourage the hope that this deficiency may soon be removed. As has already been suggested, the thousands of Mexican Americans who served the nation in the armed forces during World War II have a political consciousness that was not present in Spanish American communities prior to that time. They see now, as they did not see before, that political action is essential if their people are to rise out of second-class citizenship. It is likely that leadership will be produced by this new political ferment.

When the twenty-sixth New Mexico Legislature opened in January, 1962, the *Albuquerque Journal* listed by name the state's 32 senators and 66 members of its House of Representatives. Surnames are certainly no infallible index as to

---

[12] *Summary of Conference on Latin-American Relations, op. cit.*, p. 9.

ethnic background. Nevertheless, it was interesting to note that of the 32 senators, 8 (25 per cent) had Spanish surnames. And of the 66 representatives, 18 (27 per cent) had Spanish surnames. Since New Mexico has a Spanish American population of roughly 40 per cent, it is probable that Spanish American representation in state government in New Mexico is less than what it should be on a numerical basis. But it is also evident that in this regard, Spanish Americans are not excluded from New Mexico political life. And, in passing, we might note that in this particular, Spanish Americans have a superior position to that of Negroes, who have in no state such direct political representation. But whereas there are more Spanish Americans than Negroes in state governments, Negroes have wielded their numerical strength more effectively than Spanish Americans in national politics.

The cultural ferment among Puerto Ricans in New York City may also be a nest out of which Spanish American leadership will come in the next generation. Studies of the emergence of immigrant groups from the sociological ghetto and from second-class citizenship reveal a loose, but interesting, pattern. The pattern is not firm or consistent enough to form the basis for a theory of acculturation, but since it has occurred among the Irish, Italians, Jews, and Negroes, we should not be surprised if it occurs also among Puerto Ricans, Cubans, and Mexican Americans.

According to this loose pattern, the first emergence of the excluded minority is through some form of entertainment— the short route to wealth and popularity. By entertainment we mean the broad gamut from sports to the arts, including the theater, movies, and television. All of the minority groups mentioned above broke into this area of American life successfully years ago. The second giant step in the rise of the minority is the invasion of the political life of the nation—at the ward level first, and then in the wider political realm. The Irish, Italians, Jews, and Negroes have taken this step. In 1960 we elected our first Roman Catholic, Irish-lineage president. The line from John L. Sullivan, world champion heavyweight boxer, to John F. Kennedy, president of the United States, is a long and circuitous one, but there is a sociological connection between the two in the history of the Irish minority in this country. Similarly, there are Jews, Italians, and Negroes in high and honored governmental posts, and preceding them are Jews, Italians, and Negroes who escaped from the sociological ghetto through the entertainment world. There are signs that the Puerto Rican community in the United States is moving into the first stage of his pattern, and that—more rapidly than it happened with other minorities—political leadership will soon rise among these people. Already there is among them an emerging middle and professional class that justifies this optimistic prediction.

. . .   *Education*

We have taken sufficient note of the Spanish American's low level of employment and of the part prejudice and discrimination play in subordinating him to unskilled and semi-skilled types of work. We have noted also that, in the main, he and his family are relegated to substandard housing in urban and rural slums. In addition to these glaring deficiencies in Spanish American life, there are three others that must be noted. The first of these is the lack of adequate education. The American of Mexican and Cuban descent and, though much less so, of Puerto Rican descent, is woefully undereducated. Among Mexican Americans, the rate of literacy is very low. Because the labor of the children is needed to lift the level of the family income, many of the children, despite compulsory school attendance laws, never finish the third grade. This is particularly true of the children of Mexican American migrants, whose education is

spotty at best. In addition to the parents' need and sometimes their willingness to put the children into the fields as
soon as possible, there is a language difficulty that the public
schools, with a serious shortage of bilingual teachers, cannot
handle. Thrust from a Spanish-speaking environment into
an English-speaking school, the Mexican American child
has a crippling disadvantage. This handicap is not suffered
by Puerto Rican children to anything like the same degree.
Under the present government in Puerto Rico, the level of
public school education has risen phenomenally. It has been
said, and is probably true, that education is the single most
important need of Mexican Americans.

The problem is not that the Mexican American is incapable of being educated. If all external circumstances are
equalized, he is just as capable as any other child. He has the
same native ability and the same receptivity. The problem is
the inability of the Mexican American child to *get* an education. In most instances, the external circumstances defeat
him before he gets started. Federal aid to public school
education, a rigid enforcement of compulsory school attendance regulations, and an adequate wage that would make it
unnecessary for migrant workers to farm out their children,
would relieve some of those external circumstances that
blight the education of Mexican Americans. Adult education programs by the state, the church, and other institutions would correct this tragic situation still further and
would conserve and utilize the Mexican American capability
that is now being wasted.

· · ·   *Health*

The second deficiency is concerned with health.
Given a group of people with poor housing, low income, and
inadequate education, one would expect to find in that group
an exceptional amount of disease and a high mortality rate.
That is precisely what one does find among Spanish Amer-

icans. "Undernourishment, a high infant mortality rate, and a greater prevalence of some infectious and contagious diseases, notably tuberculosis and dysentery, are conditions frequently reported among the Spanish-speaking populations that have been studied. Age-specific birth and death rates are both somewhat higher for the Spanish-speaking than for the population as a whole, although the death rates have been coming down rather rapidly in recent years. . . ." [13] Statistics from Texas reveal that in that state the deaths from tuberculosis per 100,000 people, a few years ago, were 40 for Anglo-Americans, 50 for Negroes, and 160 for Spanish Americans. These startling contrasts are a direct result of the poverty-stricken life of the average Spanish American.

Although her sampling was limited, Dr. Beatrice Bishop Berle in her study, *80 Puerto Rican Families in New York City*, draws an applicable conclusion: "Nevertheless, the data on the eighty Puerto Rican families in this study, the clinical impression of physicians who treat Puerto Rican patients, the high incidence of new cases of tuberculosis (Lowell 1955 and 1956) and the high admission rate to mental hospitals (Malzberg 1956) reported for Puerto Ricans suggest that the general susceptibility to illness is high among Puerto Ricans in New York City as compared to other segments of the metropolitan population." [14]

. . .   *The Gospel*

Food and shelter are the irreducible physical necessities of human life. Beyond these necessities, and the financial means by which to secure them, man needs acceptance by other men, particularly by the established and the secure.

---

[13] Saunders, Lyle. *Cultural Difference and Medical Care: The Case of the Spanish-Speaking People of the Southwest*, p. 76. New York: Russell Sage Foundation, 1954.
[14] Berle, Beatrice Bishop. *80 Puerto Rican Families in New York City*, pp. 202-203. New York: Columbia University Press, 1958.

He needs organization and leadership for his community life, education for his mind, and health for his body. In all of these basic necessities of life, Spanish Americans in the United States are grossly deficient. The superficial observer assumes that at least these people have an adequate religious life and that, since they are Roman Catholics, Protestants do not have to be concerned about their moral and spiritual welfare. This assumption is far from the truth.

Even if all Spanish Americans were devout and loyal Roman Catholics, this would not cancel the Protestant obligation to offer them the evangelical gospel—present and eternal salvation through faith in God's act for all men in Jesus Christ. This is the gospel, and the sweet spirit of ecumenicity—desirable as Christian unity is—cannot alter the fact that the Roman Catholic Church has not offered this gospel to the Spanish-speaking world. We do not believe and we cannot say of the Roman Catholic Spanish American that he is adequately churched until he knows and accepts the saving power of God in Jesus Christ. Protestant attempts to evangelize Spanish Americans will not be viewed with favor by the Roman Catholic Church. Such Protestant efforts will be derided and resisted as proselytizing, and as a needless tampering with the inherited faith of these people. But upon Protestants has been laid the imperative to preach and teach the gospel of Jesus Christ to all men. Disfavor cannot cancel that imperative.

The fact, of course, is that great numbers of Spanish Americans are not devout Roman Catholics. In the first place, there is good ground for concluding that the religion many people inherited from a Mexican, Cuban, or Puerto Rican background is not Christian and is not Roman Catholic. Ernest Gruening went so far as to say: "The Mexican people are not Catholics." [15] By this he meant that through the

---

[15] Gruening, Ernest. *Mexico and Its Heritage*, p. 229. New York & London: The Century Co., 1928.

centuries of Mexican history, the blending of Roman
Catholicism and the indigenous Indian religions produced
in Mexico a new kind of faith, a faith that in its buildings
and ritual wears the façade of Catholicism but that in the
practices of the people preserves many Indian superstitions.
To a less obvious and less dramatic degree, there were similar
developments in Cuba and Puerto Rico. Many of the people who call themselves Roman Catholics practice spiritism.

When Mexicans take up residence in the United States,
their religion loses some of its paganism, but it also loses
much of its zeal. Church membership becomes nominal; the
church serves them for baptisms, marriages, fiestas, and
burials, but it has little additional significance or influence
upon their lives. Mexican Americans maintain a formal tie
with the church, think and speak of themselves as Roman
Catholics, attend church on rare occasion; but neither the
church nor its teaching plays any central or influential role
in their lives. In 1930, Manuel Gamio observed that "it is
clear that a large part of the Mexican immigrants abandon
Catholicism." [16] What is left is a vacuum, which neither Roman Catholics nor Protestants are filling. What is left is a
people without a religion. Roman Catholic authorities have
themselves confessed that the Roman Catholic Church is
reaching effectively only 10 per cent of the Spanish-speaking
people of the Southwest. Certainly, Protestants are doing
even less. There is no need for rancor, envy, resentment, and
competition between Protestants and Roman Catholics: the
field is big enough for both branches of the Christian faith.

Religious statistics on Puerto Ricans in the United States
are paltry. Roman Catholics claim that 90 per cent of them
are Roman Catholics. The Reverend David Barry of the
New York City Mission Society estimates that "one out of

---

[16] Gamio, Manuel. *Mexican Immigration to the United States,* pp.
117-118. The University of Chicago Press, 1930. Copyright 1950 by
the University of Chicago.

every five or six Puerto Ricans coming to the United States has a Protestant background." These contradictory figures reflect not only inadequate data but also some indecision on the part of the immigrants and the ease with which many of them maintain dual or multiple church memberships. They attend Roman Catholic mass, Protestant services, and spiritualist meetings with no sense of disloyalty. It has been reliably estimated that 75 per cent of the Puerto Ricans in the United States attend no church at all. Since many of the Cuban refugees are from the upper and middle classes, which are more strongly attached to the Roman Catholic Church than is the lower, rural class, perhaps the percentage of unchurched Cubans in the United States is lower than that of the Puerto Ricans. In any event, a rough, summary estimate indicates that of the five and a half million Spanish Americans in the United States, four million are detached from any church. The dimension of the task and the opportunity for the Protestant churches are both startling and demanding. We shall note later in more detail the ramifications of this need and the opportunity that it presents.

◂§ 4 SPANISH AMERICAN
CHARACTERISTICS

.   .   .   *A Necessary Precaution*

Attempts to characterize a whole people are extremely hazardous. Even according to physical description, people who are commonly thought of as one show such varieties that it is impossible to catalogue all of them with one set of anthropological definitions. American Negroes, for example, have in their group so many degrees of pigmentation, of hair texture, of bone structure, of coloration that it is difficult to portray the average Negro American. When the attempt to characterize moves into the more subtle realms of thought patterns, emotional qualities, and habitual practices, generalization becomes even more dangerous. The temptation to conclude that all members of a particular ethnic group are just like the one member we know, or to assume that every member of the group will wear all the general marks of the group, is almost irresistible. We know one person in the group and leap to the conclusion that we know all; we have a general view of all and therefore think that we know each one. Such generalizing and stereotyping is always inaccurate and is usually unjust.

Nevertheless, a loose classification of peoples is possible, and if certain rules are observed, can be accurate, just, and valuable. One rule is that all people in their basic intellectual and emotional structure are the same, even though that essential human endowment may have various expressions. There is no radical difference in the mental and emotional endowments of ethnic groups, however great the differences within the groups. To speak of Negro rhythm or Scotch thrift or the Jewish mind as though in these particulars these people were radically different from other people is an error. People are people and, despite infinite variations, are the same in their elemental structure. The fact that a person is Japanese, Indian, or Spanish American does not tell us what he is in his inner being or how he will respond to a given situation. Each may express the desire in his own way, but the Occidental and the Oriental have an equal and identical desire to "save face." This being true, it is always best to deal with people as people and not as representatives of particular groups. The hearts of men everywhere recognize one another and affirm men's basic kinship, and this oneness is much stronger and more persistent than their differences.

The second rule is that history and environment as they play upon a given group of people tend to develop in those people certain characteristics that remain dormant or less developed in other people who are under the influence of a different set of circumstances. This, indeed, is what we mean when we speak of ethnic groups. We do not mean that the people of one group are all alike and all basically different from the people of another group. We mean, rather, that climate, geography, their neighbors, and the fortunes and misfortunes of their history have developed in a certain group of people certain traits and customs that, in a general way, are common to this group. In broad, loose terms, these people can on the basis of these common traits and customs be classified as distinct from other peoples.

The third rule is that value judgments should not be made on the basis of these broad, loose classifications. The goal of the classification is understanding, not the assigning of merits and demerits. To say that the English are superior to the Spanish, the Occidental superior to the Oriental, the white to other races is to ignore the vast range of abilities and accomplishments found within every racial and ethnic group, and to discount the observable fact that in every group there are those members who are in every respect superior to some members of other groups. Whether it is boastful or derogatory, a sentence about racial and cultural and national groups which begins with the word *all*, or with its implication, should be viewed with suspicion.

The fourth rule is that no racial or ethnic group is ever truly homogeneous. However closely knit a people may be, and however isolated from other cultural streams, there remains in the group a wide latitude of individual traits that destroy perfect and complete homogeneity. This is true even of such isolated ethnic groups as the Eskimos, the Ainus of Japan, and the Pygmies of central Africa. It is even truer of those cultural and racial streams that have been exposed to other cultural and racial streams for a long period of time. A constant cross-fertilization breaks up the racial and cul-

tural consistency of the group and produces within the group
those members who do not in personal traits and habits fit
the general description.

With these rules warning us of the dangers of stereotypes
and generalizations, we can now explore Spanish American
characteristics. Let us remember as we do so that Spanish
Americans are people just like any other people, with the
same basic physical needs, the same emotional and mental
dispositions, the same hopes and fears and yearnings, the
same elemental human dispositions found in any people. But
we shall rightly expect that a particular environment and a
unique history have developed among them certain distinctive customs and transformed some of the qualities that they
share with all men into discernible traits. As we note those
cultural habits and personal characteristics that give distinctiveness to Spanish Americans, we will resist the conclusion
that these qualities make Spanish Americans either superior
or inferior to other ethnic groups. We are not engaging in
odious comparisons. Nor shall we expect uniformity in a
people as heterogeneous as Spanish Americans. Moreover,
we must confine our attention exclusively to those distinctive qualities of Spanish American life that have particular
significance for the Protestant churches in their increasing
interest in and their deepening concern for these five and a
half million, largely unchurched, Americans. We are not
attempting here a deep and definitive study of Spanish
American life.

No matter how revolutionary the development of a people
may be, they never escape their past. The violent revolutions
in France, Turkey, Russia, and other countries shattered
existing situations and sharply redirected the histories of
these nations; but in each of these nations a large part of
the past survived the national upheaval. This has been particularly true of those Spanish American nations that in the
Western Hemisphere have contributed emigrants to the

United States. They have had their political, and to a much less extent their industrial, revolutions, but the peoples' links to their Spanish, Indian, and African origins are unbroken. The cultural inheritances have been greatly modified through the passing centuries and through the merging of distinct traditions. The average Mexican today is not at home when he visits Spain or when he visits a remote Indian village in Mexico. He is a descendant of both and yet alien to both. But he, like his Cuban and Puerto Rican cousins, has in his culture and in himself the indelible marks of Spanish, Indian, and, in some cases, African cultures that have merged through the years to create a culture that is neither Spanish, Indian, nor African, but Spanish American.

When the people of this Spanish American culture entered the United States by immigration or by annexation, they met another culture—the Anglo-American. This culture is also a hybrid, the product of the interaction of several ethnic and two principal racial strains through nearly four centuries of common history. Though the people of these two cultures are basically the same, their customs and some of their dominant personality traits are different. It is folly, and it can be tragic, for the Protestant churches—which are part of and at home in the Anglo-American culture—to ignore these differences in their approach to Spanish Americans. It is even greater folly and greater tragedy for the Protestant churches to insist that Spanish Americans become Anglo-Americans in order to or as they become Protestants. To ignore the differences is to blunder into an irreparable alienation of Spanish Americans from Protestantism and from the Christian gospel as Protestants see it. To insist, even by the subtlest implication, that Spanish Americans must surrender their cherished customs and their cultural traits adds to the blunder of ignorance, deeply offends the Spanish American, and wastes the valuable contributions that the Spanish American mind and spirit can contribute to

Protestantism and to an emerging culture, which will be neither Spanish nor Negro nor Anglo-American but, eventually, simply American.

Culture is something more than costume, diet, and architecture. As Paul A. F. Walter, Jr. defines it: "Culture is the learned ways of acting and thinking which are transmitted by group members and which provide for each individual ready-made and tested solutions for vital life problems." [1] These learned ways of acting and thinking create a "cultural chasm," which has to be bridged when two peoples are brought together in one nation. In Chapter III of his book *Cultural Difference and Medical Care: The Case of the Spanish-Speaking People of the Southwest*, Lyle Saunders analyzes the "cultural chasm" between Spanish and Anglo-Americans, stressing the differences in seven areas: (1) language, (2) orientation to time, (3) attitudes toward change, (4) attitudes toward work and efficiency, (5) attitudes of acceptance and resignation, (6) attitudes toward personal dependency, and (7) attitudes toward formal organization. Readers who want to explore the cultural differences more extensively can turn to this book and to others listed in the bibliography. Our interest in this study focuses on those aspects of cultural difference that have a specifically religious significance.

.   .   .   *From Village to City*

Studies of Spanish American life have in the past made much of the fact that it is a village folk-culture and cannot be understood if this setting is disregarded. This is still true despite the migration of a majority of Spanish Americans from small rural towns to cities. The population shift is so recent that most Spanish Americans, like other Americans

---

[1] Walter, Paul A. F., Jr. *Race and Culture Relations*, p. 17. New York: McGraw-Hill Book Co., Inc., 1952. Copyright 1952, McGraw-Hill Book Co., Inc. Used by permission.

from similar backgrounds, still reflect in their relocation patterns of thought and action impressed upon them by rural communities. They cannot help bringing with them to the city some of the mores and most of the attitudes learned in the village. The clashing of this village folk-culture against the ways and the attitudes of men in the city produces serious problems of adjustment for Spanish Americans and their new neighbors, and equally serious problems inside Spanish American families.

There is a great deal of similarity between Spanish Americans who move to the city and mountaineers who move to industrial centers from the Southern Appalachians. In both cases the life from which they move is rural or semirural, relatively low geared in its activities, isolated from the main currents of American life, permissive of rugged individuality, close to the soil, simply organized. But there is also a striking difference between these two migrating peoples. Whereas Southern mountaineers are an eddy in the Anglo-American culture, Spanish American farmers and villagers bring the mainstream of Spanish American culture into American life and into its cities. The eddy is more easily rechanneled and blended with the flowing Anglo-American history than is the competing stream. Or, said differently, it is much easier for Southern mountaineers to adjust to metropolitan America than it is for Spanish Americans to do so. To the new environment to which they come, and to the new environment that pushes in upon them, Spanish Americans present patterns of family life and attitudes about themselves, their work, their government, their religion that are distinctly their own rather than Anglo-American.

. . .   *The Family Pattern*

Traditional Spanish American family life is being challenged and to some extent shattered by modern, industrial America, but in its classic structure it was hierarchical rather than democratic. It assumed dominance by the male members of the home, with the father the actual as well as titular head of the family. His authority was supreme but was shared by his sons in degrees that descended from the oldest to the youngest. As the dominant member of the family, the father enjoyed special privileges: a social life with his male friends apart from his home and a double standard of morality binding his wife to the marriage vows but liberating him. The woman's role, subordinate to the man's, kept the mother in the home and the daughters sequestered. The wife was expected to be faithful to her husband, restricted except on rare occasions to a social life within the home, loyal to the church. There were no intermediate steps between the good wife and the bad woman. Girls were closely chaperoned and were never alone with their escorts even after they became engaged. In this patriarchal family system, contrary to what an Anglo-American would expect, there developed strong family ties and a tightly knit home life. Large families, autocratic fathers, romanticized mothers, sequestered daughters, and a pervasive spirit of family oneness—these were the marks of classical Spanish American family life.

This view of family life remains strong in the older generations of Spanish Americans. Fathers still try to rule their families as their fathers did before them. Mothers still expect for themselves and for their daughters the traditional subordinate role. But the younger generation is rebelling against this inherited family structure. Grown men who are still unmarried and who still live with their parents declare their independence and withdraw from the intimate communal life of the family. Adolescent Spanish American girls are rebelling with increasing success against seclusion and the chaperon and are meeting young men outside and in their homes in defiance of Spanish American traditions and the disapproval of their parents. These changes break a cherished continuity with the past, baffle the older generation, and produce tensions and open conflicts between parents and children.

The Reverend Merrill O. Young of St. Augustine's Chapel in New York City indicated in a group discussion some of the ramifications of this conflict:

One of the problems that intensifies this inter-generation difficulty is that the standards of behavior of children in Puerto Rico are quite different from what they are here. The Spanish parents expect from their children a standard of behavior which just doesn't exist. They get very tense and frightened when their child is behaving like a perfectly good New York child, because he isn't behaving like a good Puerto Rican child. It seems to me that this conflict of the standards which the children pick up from the city and the standards which their parents have for them produces awfully shattering situations very early.[2]

The classical and now seriously challenged pattern of Spanish American family life differs from the modern Anglo-American pattern not so much in kind or degree as it does in timing. Fifty years ago in the southern parts of the United States—even today, in some remote, secluded areas of that region—the hierarchical, male-dominated family pattern was the rule. Under the impact of education, urbanization, and industrialization the family structure was loosened, home life was democratized, and women were liberated. Still earlier, the same process occurred in the northern and eastern parts of the United States. Today, the same history that revolutionized Anglo-American family life is catching up with Spanish Americans and is creating for them the same problems of adjustment experienced by Anglo-Americans in the earlier days of American history.

The strong Spanish American sense of family is both exclusive and inclusive—exclusive in its sequestering and pro-

---

[2] *Summary of Conference on Problems of Puerto Ricans in the United States*, p. 18. Home Department, The National Council of the Protestant Episcopal Church, 1962.

tecting of the female members of the family, yet inclusive
in the maintenance of ties with distant relatives and with
"adopted" relatives. In the address mentioned in Chapter 3,
Ralph L. Beals commented on the strength of familial ties
in Spanish American culture: "These are further extended
by an extraordinary flowering of pseudo-kinship ties, the
compadrazgo. God-parents are chosen for every conceivable
occasion and the more important are treated substantially as
members of the extended family. In small communities, it
often happens that almost everyone stands in some kinship
or pseudo-kinship relation to almost everyone else." [3] This
craving for community should be of particular interest to the
Protestant churches in their appeal to Spanish Americans.
Here is a need that the churches can help meet and a
strength that Protestant churches can use.

.   .   .   *Attitudes Toward Work*

When the Spanish American and the Anglo-American cultures meet, two opposite and conflicting views of the
nature and purpose of work collide. Anglo-Americans, including the large number of Roman Catholics who have
absorbed or deliberately adopted the Protestant concept of
work, generally believe that work is a virtue, an end in itself.
Max Weber, R. H. Tawney, and others have argued that
capitalism with its emphasis upon enterprise, individuality,
and the accumulation of material goods is a product of the
Protestant Reformation. This probably puts the case too
strongly, but undoubtedly, the Protestant ethic gives to work
in and of itself a sanction that Roman Catholicism does not
give. To our Puritan ancestors, industry and thrift were
virtues in themselves; idleness was sinful and leisure a temptation.

---

[3] From Ralph L. Beals's 1951 address to the Fifth Annual Conference
of the Southwest Council on the Education of Spanish-Speaking People,
George Pepperdine College, Los Angeles, California.

Spanish Americans were nurtured on the contrary view that work is a means to an end, not a virtue but an honorable necessity. Whether we credit that view to Roman Catholicism, to the centuries-old way of life practiced by the Spanish Americans' Indian ancestors, to the tropical climate, or to some other source, it is the general Spanish American view of work. This concept of work as a necessity rather than a virtue is not unique with Spanish Americans; but the significant fact for us is that it is real, is deep in Spanish American consciousness, and is directly opposite to the view generally held by Anglo-Americans. For the Spanish American, the value of work is its power to produce the desired things of life: the necessities and the extras that make life possible and enjoyable. And one of the values that the Spanish American wants work to produce is surcease from work, a leisure in which life can be savored.

The possibility for misunderstanding is great when these opposite and conflicting views meet. The Spanish American cannot understand the zeal and fervor of Anglo-American enterprise, nor can he adjust himself easily to the pace and pressure of a work-centered civilization. He concludes that the Anglo-American is money mad, that his Anglo-American boss is a hard taskmaster, that the Anglo-American has no interest in the finer things of life. From his side, the Anglo-American is liable to conclude that the Spanish American is indolent, procrastinating, or insufficiently dedicated to his job. What Robert J. Alexander said about the misunderstandings that rise from the chasm between North Americans and Latin Americans can be applied with some modification to the void that exists between Spanish American and Anglo-American attitudes toward work:

Both North Americans and the Latin-Americans tend to misunderstand and underestimate the other's cultural achievements. Yankee as a semi-barbarian, very capable in the production and The Latin Americans often think in terms of the "materialistic" manipulation of gadgets but without any "soul" and with little or no interest in the finer things of life. For their part, the North Americans tend to regard their Latin American neighbors as "romantic," somewhat shiftless, and utterly unsophisticated. They seldom think of them as having any particular interest or ability in arts and letters, or in the physical or social sciences.[4]

Obviously, the views that Spanish Americans and Anglo-Americans have of each other because of their contrary attitudes toward work are stereotypes. In each group there are people who fit the stereotypes—who are materialistic, money-mad worshipers of work, or who are lazy, shiftless ne'er-do-wells. But neither view describes a whole people. In particular, we can say that if the Spanish American philosophy of work made men indolent, then the United States would not have imported hundreds of thousands of Mexicans and Puerto Ricans and turned over to them the most menial, tedious, back breaking jobs the nation has to offer. On the contrary, these people were lured across the border because, though they do not accept work as one of life's ultimates, they do accept work as the lot of man and as a personal necessity. The Anglo-American's picture of the Spanish American lolling in the shade of a huge sombrero waiting for mañana is false and unjust.

. . .   *Notions of Class and Kind*

Since the stratifying of societies is a universal cultural characteristic, it should not surprise Anglo-Americans to discover that Spanish Americans have a strong class consciousness. This is obviously not a Spanish American distinctive, but since Anglo-Americans tend to think of Spanish Americans in collective terms and as a homogeneous people, it needs to be noted here that closed-class systems operated for

---

[4] From *Today's Latin America,* by Robert J. Alexander. Copyright © 1962 by Robert J. Alexander. Reprinted by permission of Doubleday & Co., Inc.

centuries in Mexico, Puerto Rico, and Cuba, and that though these systems are breaking down, each immigrant from these countries brings with him a strong identity with a particular stratum of society. The Anglo-American who ignores this fact in dealing with a class-conscious immigrant, especially if that immigrant considers himself in the middle or upper class, will embarrass both himself and the immigrant. This danger is particularly acute in the case of Anglo-Americans who view Spanish Americans with contempt or with condescension.

The second danger is that Anglo-Americans apply their own standards of class structure to Spanish Americans and expect Spanish American society to follow in its divisions the traditional lines of American segregation—race and color. But these are not the standards of social classification among Spanish Americans. Neither Mexicans, Puerto Ricans, nor Cubans accept skin color as an ultimate basis of social division. Although Spanish Americans are color conscious, light colored skin does not automatically win preferred status; dark colored skin is not an automatic mark of inferiority. Spanish Americans who have for a long time been exposed to American racial prejudice may absorb it, but it is not a native form of prejudice. In the main, status among Spanish Americans has nothing to do with pigmentation; theirs is a class rather than a race consciousness. In this respect, they are different from Anglo-Americans, who have both a class and a race consciousness. It is well for Protestants, both Negro and white, to keep these facts clearly in mind in dealing with Spanish Americans: they have a strong class sense, but it has little to do with color.

.   .   .   *The Individual*

It is patently impossible for an Anglo-American to analyze and describe the soul of a Spanish American and thereby to indicate the ways in which environment and his-

tory have developed in him personality traits different from
those of the Anglo-American. Such description is better done
from the inside out, in confession, than it is from the outside
in, by analysis. Such confessions are available, and few of
them—if an Anglo-American can be the judge—are superior
to that of Samuel Ramos, a professor of social philosophy
and aesthetic theory in the National University of Mexico a
generation ago. In his confession, Ramos speaks, of course,
for himself and for Mexicans; but what he confesses speaks
as well for Spanish Americans of Mexican extraction living
now in the United States.

In his book *Profile of Man and Culture in Mexico*,[5] Ramos
makes two points that give us insights into Spanish American personality. First, Ramos stresses Mexican religiosity:
"The real motivation for our culture, given the nature of our
psychic activity since the time of the Conquest, is religiosity.
. . . In other words, one can say that Mexican history, especially in its spiritual sense, is a matter of the affirmation or
negation of religious sentiment. Whichever branch of our
ascendancy is considered—that of the Indian or that of the
Spanish conqueror—the most notable resultant characteristic
is our exalted religiosity."[6] He stresses the fact that the
whole history of the Mexican people—intellectual as well as
artistic—is "a variation on the theme of spiritualism."[7]
Those Spanish American characteristics that Anglo-Americans tend to dismiss as romantic, sentimental, poetic, this
Mexican author describes as basically a consuming and per-
vading religious attitude toward life. It can even be shown
that the defiance of religion, the cults of Spanish American
atheism, the rebellions against the church are expressions
of the Mexican's intense spirituality and his repudiation of

[5] Ramos, Samuel. *Profile of Man and Culture in Mexico*. Translated
by Peter G. Earle. Austin: University of Texas Press, 1962. (Published
in Spanish in 1934.)

[6] *Ibid.*, p. 77.

[7] *Ibid.*, p. 89.

mechanistic concepts of life. Whether or not he is formally religious, the Mexican's whole being, says Ramos, oozes religiosity.

This description of the basic quality of Mexican personality can be borrowed as a generally true, if somewhat less precise, description of the profile of Spanish American personality. It is not enough to picture the Spanish American as an incurable romantic, as a sentimentalist. He must be seen as one who—to the extent that he is uncorrupted by the common sense, practical, mechanistic Anglo-American philosophy—views all life through religious eyes. We shall return later to this description in considering how the Protestant with a different orientation and with a personality molded by a different set of circumstances can make the appeal of his faith to, and can profit from, the Spanish American's domination by a religious motivation that governs his whole being. We stress here the important fact that though the great majority of Spanish Americans are unchurched, they are not unreligious.

Second, in his analysis of the Mexican, Ramos states that the Mexican suffers from a feeling of inferiority and exhibits that feeling in what the psychologist Adler termed "the virile protest." Ramos makes the very important distinction that the Mexican is not really inferior but only feels inferior. This, of course, is a generalization about Mexicans that Ramos drew from his study of the *pelado*, the lowest stratum of urban society in Mexico. His categorization suffers from the liabilities of all generalizations, but there is much in the author and in his thesis to commend his insight when he says that "the Mexican psyche is the result of reactions that strive to conceal an inferiority complex." [8] Mexican self-denigration in its extreme *pelado* form expresses itself, as Ramos sees it, in "a constant irritability," "a sentiment of hostility," in exaggerated boasts of virility and masculinity. The higher

---

[8] *Ibid.*, p. 58.

the cultural level, the more refined this mood becomes and the more subtly it expresses itself.

It would be inaccurate to say that the Spanish American in the United States is nothing more than a transplanted Mexican. The Puerto Ricans, Cubans, and the Mexican Americans who have lived in the present bounds of the United States for centuries would be quick and justified in pointing out such a gross error. But it is correct to say that Ramos' profile of the Mexican gives us insight into the psychology of most Spanish Americans living in the United States. His fundamental description of the Mexican mood is a partial description—or, perhaps better said, a partial explanation—of a distinctive, though not necessarily universal, Spanish American psychology.

Allowing for exceptions and for varying degrees of appropriateness, we can say that most Spanish Americans have a strong sense of personal dignity. No matter how low the individual Spanish American may be on the social ladder, he has *dignidad*; no matter how well he conceals the hurt when he is insulted, he feels deeply all affronts to his person. In this respect, Spanish Americans are certainly not unique. They have, as we have noted, no unique personality traits. But it is the degree to which the Spanish Americans hold, stress, and express *dignidad* that distinguishes them from Anglo-Americans. All people are vulnerable to insults to their person. It is neither inaccurate nor offensive to say that Spanish Americans have a particularly sharp sense of personal dignity and a low threshold of resentment to insult.

This sense of personal dignity, with its keen sensitivity to offensive words and deeds, expresses itself in a variety of ways. At the lower social levels this mood becomes an overpowering hunger for, and assertion of, physical virility, masculinity, and manliness in a basically biological sense. Adolescent Spanish American boys are particularly tempted by the urge to prove themselves manly, to sublimate feelings of inferiority by proving that they are *muy hombre*, men of spirit and courage. And, as we would expect of any people, some Spanish American men never outgrow this adolescence. This aggressive, physical assertion of manliness lies at the root of the harm done to and by some Puerto Rican youth in New York City and by some Mexican American adolescents and young adults in Los Angeles and in other large cities of the Southwest. The collision of sensitive, self-conscious personalities and a hostile, unreceptive society will inevitably produce violence. The church will forfeit its right to serve Spanish Americans and will defeat its own purposes if it ignores the natural and legitimate hunger of these people for a sense of identity, acceptance, and personal importance.

If attack is the response of some Spanish Americans to affronts to their sense of personal dignity, withdrawal is the response of others. They isolate themselves from the rebuffs of society with a feigned indifference and aloofness. In self-protection, they repress their natural conviviality in relationships with people outside the Spanish American community, particularly with Anglo-Americans. It should not surprise Anglo-Americans if they sometimes find Spanish Americans defiant, aloof, suspicious, and distrustful. How could it be otherwise? Most Spanish Americans are descendants of a people defeated and subdued by the United States in a war that was wholly unjust and marked by unnecessary violence and cruelty. When the descendants of these defeated people came to the United States, largely at the insistence of the United States, they were viewed as interlopers, held at the lowest levels of employment, treated as second-class citizens, excluded from the main currents of American life. Such a history is not likely to produce an amiable relationship between peoples nor to cultivate in a mistreated, sensitive people an affection for, or a trust of, those who either oppress them or dismiss them indifferently.

We have obviously not attempted a sociological or psychological survey of Spanish Americans in this brief space. (Readers who want to make such a study are referred to the bibliography.) What we have done is to throw some light on those aspects of Spanish American culture that persist in a civilization dominated by an Anglo-American culture. We have given our attention to those phases of Spanish American life that are of special interest to the Protestant churches: the family pattern, attitudes of work, notions of class and kind, and individual attitudes. We shall now put to use what we have learned about the history, the life, and the personal traits of Spanish Americans as we turn in Part Two to a consideration of the problems and opportunities in ministering to Spanish Americans.

PART TWO

Ministering to Spanish Americans

5 PROTESTANTISM'S APPEAL
TO SPANISH AMERICANS

. . .   *The Myth of Incompatibility*

It is a common assumption that Protestantism and Spanish American culture are so alien to each other that they are totally incompatible and mutually exclusive. Roman Catholicism's domination of the vast areas once held by the Spanish empire is explained, not as it should be, on the basis of historical factors, but rather as the product of an intrinsic affinity of Spanish culture and Catholicism for each other. This myth insists that the spirit of the Spanish American is naturally receptive to Roman Catholicism and that this spirit is not congenial to Protestantism. This assumption is widespread and popular; it is nourished and spread by the Roman Catholic Church; it is thoughtlessly repeated by historians, journalists, sociologists, travel agents, and political scientists.

The implication drawn from this myth is that Protestant missions to Spanish Americans in the United States and abroad are an offense against the innate character of these people. It is said that when Protestants seek to win Spanish Americans, they tamper with loyalties that should not be tempted, and that when they succeed in converting Spanish Americans, they twist personalities that are happy and wholesome only when they are in the embrace of Catholi-

cism. Perpetrators of the myth think that *Spanish* means
Catholic and that to make a Spanish-speaking person Protestant is to destroy all of the Spanish qualities in his life. In
a word, the myth is used to condemn all Protestant approaches to Spanish Americans and to claim all racial and
cultural descendants of Spain for the Roman Catholic
Church. It is therefore essential that we take a look at this
myth. If it is true, as most Roman Catholics and many Protestants assume, we must take one course of action in our
ministry to Spanish Americans. If it is not true, then we must
come to the conclusion that the witness and service of the
Protestant churches to Spanish Americans should be widely
extended and intensified.

Note first that the myth of incompatibility has many able
champions. We can dismiss the claims of the Roman Catholic Church. Understandably, this church does not want its
monopoly in the Spanish-speaking world—however badly
that monopoly has been handled—threatened by opinions
that throw that world open to the evangelical churches. The
possessive attitude of the Roman Catholic Church in all dis-
cussions of the religious life of Spanish Americans does not,
of course, alter the facts—at least no more so than does the
desire of the Protestant churches to challenge the monopoly.
The utterances of both sides in such a controversy should be
viewed with suspicion. But if it is left to Roman Catholicism
to describe the relationship of the Spanish American spirit
to Roman Catholicism, it can be expected that the description will draw the relationship as tight as possible.

However, the Roman Catholic Church is not alone in
affirming the myth of Protestant-Spanish American incompatibility. Even so competent a philosopher and political
scientist as Salvador de Madariaga, one of the few liberal
Spaniards of our generation, accepts and repeats the assumption that the Protestant and Spanish American spirits are
hostile to each other. In exile from his native Spain, Sr. de

Madariaga wrote: "I do not make any bones about adding that I believe it to be a very poor service to our common civilization [Spanish-Indian] that these Indians should be taught either the Protestant faith in Spanish or the Catholic faith in English or, worst of all, a Protestant faith in English." [1] In this extraordinarily unconditional statement—so unlike his usual analysis—Sr. de Madariaga slams the door on all Protestant missions to Spanish American Indians. He believes that Indians who do not speak Spanish should be brought into the culture of their nations by teaching them Spanish but they must not be taught Protestantism in Spanish or in English. How can we explain this except to say that for Sr. de Madariaga, to be Spanish is to be Roman Catholic?

A similar description by F. S. C. Northrop assumes that there is an impassable void between South American artistry and sentiment on the one hand and Protestant drabness and stiffness on the other. He says: "A church with the diversity of vivid colors which the Indian aesthetic imagination demands would shock a Protestant congregation. But imagine, conversely, how the Protestant religion must appear to the religious Mexicans. Its exceedingly verbal preaching, its aesthetic color-blindness, and its emotional tepidity and coldness must make it look to them like no religion at all." [2] These two references are examples of a very general attitude that assumes that a Spanish American can become a Protestant only by ceasing to be a Spanish American and by a withdrawal from the community that perpetuates his ancestral traditions.

We have described a myth that is deeply infused in American thought, championed by the Roman Catholic Church,

[1] Madariaga, Salvador de. *Latin America Between the Eagle and the Bear*, pp. 62-63. New York: Frederick A. Praeger, Publisher, 1962.
[2] Northrop, F. S. C. *The Meeting of East and West*, p. 37. New York: The Macmillan Co., 1946. Reprinted by permission of the Macmillan Co.

accepted by many historians and other students of Spanish
American life, and that is a serious though not insurmount-
able obstacle to the Protestant effort to win converts among
Spanish Americans. Is the myth true? Should Protestants
leave the religious care of Spanish Americans entirely to the
Roman Catholic Church? Or is there another side to this
account, a side that not only permits but that clearly encourages a Protestant Christian evangelization of Spanish
Americans?

.   .   .   *The Fallacies of the Myth*

It is neither possible nor necessary to discount the
prestige of such champions of the myth of incompatibility as
Madariaga and Northrop. Neither is it necessary to impugn
the motives of those who gullibly accept the assumption that
Spanish culture and the Protestant temperament are mutually exclusive. But it can and should be pointed out that the
data on which this assumption is founded are inadequate
and archaic and therefore fallacious. When Northrop, for
example, writes of the "emotional tepidity and coldness" of
Protestantism, he betrays a limited knowledge of evangelical churches. There are Protestant churches that fit this description; there are even more that do not. Likewise, Madariaga accepts a common myth about Protestantism without
subjecting that myth to the correctives that a knowledge of
modern Protestantism and its success among Spanish Americans would add. Let us examine the errors in which the
myth is rooted.

First, the belief that Protestantism and Spanish Americans
are innately hostile to each other ignores the appeal that the
Protestant Reformation made to Spain and to the Spanish
soul in the sixteenth century and the subtle persistence of
that appeal to this day. The Reformation, which met a re-
sponsive spirit in Spaniards, was ruthlessly crushed by the
Spanish Inquisition. Juan de Valdés, whom the Spanish and

Roman Catholic literary critic, Menéndez y Pelayo, called
Spain's second greatest prose writer after Cervantes, was a
sixteenth century Spanish layman who came under the influence of the Reformation and whose evangelical writings
so enraged the Roman Catholic Church that he was driven
from Spain. His works were so thoroughly denounced and
suppressed by the church that they were lost to the world for
three centuries. Valdés' *Alfabeto Cristiano* and his *Diálogo
de la Doctrina Cristiana* are now listed among the classical
works of the Protestant Reformation. Juan de Valdés was
driven from Spain by the church not because his spirit and
his teachings were repulsive to Spaniards but rather because
his spirit and teachings appealed strongly to those Spaniards
who found the autocratic, spiritless church repulsive. John
A. Mackay has written in his introduction to a study of oppression of Protestants in Spain: "It is, moreover, a fact of
history, recognized by Spanish writers, that had it not been
for the very special political situation obtaining at the time,
and the extreme violence of the Inquisition, Spain would
have had her own Reformation, just as other lands in Europe
had theirs." [3]

The yearning of Spanish people for a reformation, for an
evangelical faith, though crushed in the sixteenth century,
has not entirely died. In recent years that yearning has found
expression in Spanish Roman Catholics who, though technically remaining within the church, were evangelical in
spirit. In the twentieth century the principal voice of that
yearning was that of Miguel de Unamuno, who like Juan de
Valdés suffered exile from his homeland because of his evangelical spirit and because he boldly and convincingly denied
the myth that the Spanish soul and Roman Catholicism
were inseparable. Mackay puts the point strongly: "The central trend in Spanish life and thought, the soul of the eternal

[3] Delpech, Jacques. *The Oppression of Protestants in Spain*, p. 7.
Boston: The Beacon Press, Inc., 1955.

Spain, has always rejected, and will continue to reject, the unholy wedlock between a totalitarian state and a totalitarian church, which the theorists of Hispanicism would permanently impose upon the life of a great people." [4]

Spain's greatest tragedy, a tragedy that still haunts it and blights it today, was the crushing of the Protestant Reformation in that country in the sixteenth century. The tragedy of the mother country was inherited by that country's cultural descendants in the Western world. The greatest misfortune of all Spanish America was that it fell into the hands of an autocratic state and the most decadent national division of an autocratic church. The tragedy was not so much that Roman Catholics rather than Protestants became the rulers of half the new world but that the conquered land fell under that part of the Roman Catholic Church that had been least redeemed and renewed by the Protestant Reformation. We are not forgetting the heroic, devoted, humanitarian Catholic missionaries who helped open up the new world. It was not they but the church that followed them that cut off the spirit of the Reformation from the Spanish lands of the Western Hemisphere. The benefits of the Reformation and the renewal of the Roman Catholic Church in central Europe bypassed the Roman Church in Spain; the Spanish colonies in the new world consequently suffered the same deprivations.

A survey commission authorized by the International Missionary Council reported:

What is not generally known in other parts of the world is that the Roman Catholic Church of Latin America never felt the influence of the Reformation, that it has largely retained the garb of sixteenth century Iberian fanaticism and superstition, that its popular manifestation to this day is a syncretism of Christian and Indian or African beliefs and practices, that it has pursued a policy of reaction throughout the history of inde-

---

[4] *Ibid.*, p. 10.

pendence of the Latin American countries, and has lost the respect and devotion of the people as a whole. According to one estimate made by a Roman Catholic investigator, 93 per cent of Latin Americans claim to be Catholics, but only 10 per cent actually practice the faith.[5]

Only in the last century and particularly in the last half-century have the Spanish Americans had an opportunity to decide for themselves whether they want a reformed church and an evangelical faith.

Second, the myth of Protestant-Spanish American incompatibility is rooted in the erroneous assumption that there is a correlation between the religious censuses that describe Central and South American countries as predominantly Roman Catholic and the religion actually practiced by the people of those countries. For example, Cuba was described in pre-Castro days as a Roman Catholic country, but estimates of the number of faithful, practicing Roman Catholics in Cuba, estimates made by competent observers of the Cuban scene, run as low as 3 per cent and seldom higher than 10 per cent of the population. Though nominally Roman Catholic, the great bulk of the people have no religion at all. Or, more correctly, we should say, as does W. Stanley Rycroft, secretary for research of the Commission on Ecumenical Mission and Relations of the United Presbyterian Church, that the Cubans have much religion and little faith. That is, the façade of Roman Catholicism is everywhere evident, but even a minimal loyalty to Roman Catholicism on the part of most people who adopt the Catholic title is missing. What is true of Cuba is similarly though to a lesser extent true of Mexico and Puerto Rico. The Roman Catholic Church, which for four centuries had a complete monopoly of religion in South American countries,

---

[5] Scopes, Wilfred, ed. *The Christian Ministry in Latin America and the Caribbean*, p. 25. New York: Commission on World Mission and Evangelism of the World Council of Churches, 1962.

has won to itself only a fraction of the people. The argument that the Roman Catholic Church has an exclusive claim on the religious life of all Spanish Americans is refuted by that church's four-hundred-year-old failure in meeting the moral and spiritual needs of these people. The statistics, indeed, suggest that for the great majority of the people Roman Catholicism as practiced in Latin America and the Spanish American temperament are incompatible and mutually exclusive.

The third error lies in the identification of Protestantism with Puritanism. It is held that the warm-blooded, vibrant, romantic, sentimental Spanish American mood naturally repudiates the joyless, colorless life that Protestantism indorses. There are two mistakes in this assumption. It would be true if seventeenth century Puritanism—dull, moralistic, drab, and prohibitive—were representative of Protestantism. But anyone who knows Puritanism and Protestantism knows also that Puritanism is merely one of the many streams in non-Roman Christianity. It is no more accurate or fair to describe current Protestantism in terms of colonial Puritanism than it is to describe modern Roman Catholicism in the United States in terms of sixteenth century Spain. One visit to an evangelical Spanish American church service is enough to correct this error, but most writers of Spanish American history and most analysts of Spanish American culture prefer cherished myths to discomforting facts. Spanish Americans may not find in some Protestant churches the warmth, color, excitement, and enthusiasm that they desire; but in other Protestant churches they do.

This error stems also from the generalization that holds that there is not only a distinctive but also a unique Spanish American temperament to which only the Roman Catholic Church can appeal. Further, the erroneous assumption holds that the unique Spanish American temperament is universal among these people. The notion is that the Spanish American soul is unique and that every Spanish American is just like every other Spanish American. We have seen that there are certain characteristic Spanish American traits, but it is also true that these people have the same varieties of aptitudes, appetites, artistic yearnings, and intellectual inclinations as are found in any other people. Just as they are not physically homogeneous, so they are not spiritually homogeneous. Give a group of Spanish Americans complete freedom and opportunity in selecting their churches, and some will be Roman Catholics; some Episcopalians; some Baptists, Lutherans, Methodists, Presbyterians; some Pentecostalists; some Friends; some Spiritualists; some a combination of several of these confessions; and some will have no formal religious affiliation at all.

The generalization does not hold; Spanish Americans are as varied in their reactions to ritual, liturgy, music, preaching, etc. as any other people. There is, as far as religion is concerned, no Spanish American type, no unique and universal Spanish American mood that can be satisfied only by Roman Catholicism. The Spanish American is a man, with all the variations, contradictions, eccentricities, surprises, and diverse needs suggested by that generic term. For some Spanish Americans the Roman Church is the only church, but for an increasing number of Spanish Americans a Protestant church is the preferred church.

This fact—the preference of an increasing number of Spanish Americans in the United States and throughout the Western Hemisphere for evangelical Protestantism—suggests the third error perpetuating the myth of incompatibility. The myth ignores the accelerating numbers of Spanish Americans who are breaking their nominal connection with the Roman Catholic Church and are becoming members of Protestant churches. In the short period of time in which Protestant missions have operated with some degree of freedom in South America, the Protestant population has grown to more than 4 per cent of the total population and is rising at a sharp rate. The Protestant population in Latin American countries doubled during the last ten years; the general population doubled in the last forty years—clear evidence that Protestant churches are gaining large numbers of converts from those people who are nominal Roman Catholics or who have no religious affiliation. And this, in turn, proves that Protestantism appeals to, is acceptable to, and is needed by Spanish Americans in all countries.

The Roman Catholic Church is not unaware of this development. Writing in the September 9, 1960, issue of the *Commonweal*, Father Willard F. Jabusch said, "If the Latin-American scene is carefully studied, there can no longer be any doubt that Protestantism has solidly established itself in many places and in the minds of many people has gained a reputation for sincerity, progress, and respectability." Paulus Gordan, O.S.B., editor of the Benedictine journal *Erbe und Auftrag*, is another Roman Catholic who admits that Latin American Roman Catholicism suffers from "a religious-cultural anemia." Writing in the December, 1961, issue of the Lutheran World Federation's theological quarterly, *Lutheran World*, Father Gordan, as would be expected, refutes the claim of some evangelical missionaries "that the gospel is unknown in Latin America, that it has gone under, and must therefore be proclaimed anew." But Father Gordan confesses the failures of the Roman Catholic Church in Latin America in areas of education, social reform, and pastoral ministry, admitting that these failures make "the natural point of contact for Protestant missionaries of various kinds."

Our interest in this study focuses on Spanish Americans in the United States; but if, as we see, the appeal of Protestantism to Spanish-speaking people is strong where the Roman Catholic Church has had a four-hundred-year-old monopoly and where the cliché is that to be Spanish is to be

Roman Catholic, then the appeal of Protestantism to Spanish Americans will be even stronger in the pluralistic, democratic society of the United States. The journey from Roman Catholicism to Protestantism is much shorter, much less hazardous in terms of psychic and family perils, in a country that is still nominally and culturally Protestant than it could possibly be in countries where the religious life of the people has been traditionally and politically entrusted to the Roman Church.

.   .   .   *Varieties of Appeal and Response*

The response of Spanish Americans to the appeal of Protestantism invites erroneous oversimplification. We are tempted to conclude on the basis of abstract reasoning that all Spanish Americans will react in a specific way to the evangelizing efforts of Protestant churches. Likewise, if we know a specific situation, we are disposed to make that situation descriptive of the whole Spanish American response to the Protestant appeal. On the basis of such abstract reasoning and by generalizing from particulars, we fall into the following erroneous characterizations. We may succumb, as we have noted, to the myth and conclude that a deep interpenetration of Spanish American culture and Roman Catholicism precludes the conversion of Spanish Americans to the evangelical faith. Or through similar reasoning we may assume that when Spanish Americans become Protestants they all gravitate toward those denominations that in their worship have a pageantry and a liturgy similar to that of the Roman Catholic Church. Acquainted with some Spanish American family that as a part of its religious discipline abstains from smoking, movies, and light literature, we may imagine that all Spanish American Protestants flee from the relative moral laxity of Spanish Catholicism to Protestant Puritanism. News about the popularity of Pentecostal sects in some Spanish American communities may deceive us into believing that most evangelical Spanish Americans prefer an "allelujah" kind of religion. From limited data we may conclude, as John H. Burma did, that "Protestants tend to be in the middle rather than at either extreme of the Mexican-American socioeconomic scale." [6]

There is truth in each of these statements, but as generalizations they are erroneous and misleading. Whether for good or for ill, Spanish Americans who become Protestants enter all the varieties of American Protestantism. The religious taste of the Spanish American is not Roman Catholic but catholic with a small "c." The inclinations of Spanish Americans in worship, in church polity, and in personal discipline are universal inclinations, as many and as varied as are found among any other people. The responses of Spanish Americans to the appeal of Protestantism is not one-directional but as varied as the multiple facets of Protestantism. The response includes total repudiation on the one extreme and fanatical devotion on the other and touches all the gradations in between.

The role of the Protestant churches in their mission to Spanish Americans is not vindictive or competitive. The purpose is not to compete with or to harm the Roman Catholic Church. Some devout Roman Catholic Spanish Americans will, of course, become Protestants when they hear and understand the evangelical witness, but an even larger number of these Christians will undoubtedly remain loyal Roman Catholics. The fact is that the vast majority of Spanish Americans are unchurched and that they constitute a mission field that may easily exhaust all the resources and the manpower of both Roman Catholics and Protestants.

At the same time the role of Protestant churches is not restricted to unchurched Spanish Americans. Spanish-speak-

---

[6] Burma, John H. *Spanish-Speaking Groups in the United States*, pp. 83-84. Durham: Duke University Press, 1954.

ing people, even those who are devout Roman Catholics, are not a sacred preserve from which all Protestant witness is excluded. On the contrary, Protestants believe that they have a gospel that Roman Catholics need. If the proclaiming of that gospel to Roman Catholics subjects Protestants to the charge that they are proselytizing, this is a charge that they accept with joy. This is exactly what they are trying to do—to convert all men to a simple faith in God through Jesus Christ and through him alone. In the process, Protestants must make sure that they act without malice toward and indulge in no false witness against the Roman Catholic Church. They must bear their witness to Jesus Christ in the power and in the spirit of Jesus Christ. In obedience to the command of that Christ, the Protestant churches must serve the needs and minister to the spiritual hungers of Spanish-speaking Americans. The churches, testifying in word and deed to the salvation offered all men in Jesus Christ, must give Spanish Americans the long-delayed blessing of the Reformation: every man's opportunity to decide for himself how directly and voluntarily he will serve God and glorify his name and every man's assurance that he has salvation through the grace of God freely given in Jesus Christ to all who receive him. Questions of class, race, wealth, social status, cultural background, traditions, and inherited religion are irrelevant; the role of the Protestant churches is to proclaim the saving grace of God as it is known to those churches solely in Jesus Christ. No ethnic group in the United States has a greater need for, and promises a more grateful response to, the Protestant testimony and to offers of Protestant community than do Spanish Americans. And, at the same time, Protestantism in the United States cannot be true to itself and meet its own continual need for renewal if it withholds that testimony and that community from Spanish Americans.

∞§ 6 WHAT THE CHURCHES
ARE DOING

. . .   *Inadequate Statistics*

Church membership statistics are notoriously unreliable, and numerical descriptions of Spanish American
Protestants are especially fragmentary and untrustworthy
even when they are issued by the most responsible and con-
scientious sources. The reasons for the spotty statistical reports on Spanish American Protestants are several: the lack
of precise censuses of Mexican Americans in the fluid area
along the Mexican border and of Puerto Ricans in a similarly
turbulent population in New York City, the easy flow of
many Spanish Americans from one church to another and
back again, the casualness with which some of them hold
simultaneous membership in several churches, the rise and
fall of numerous storefront churches in the New York City
area, the elusiveness of migrant families and their aversion to
inquiries that seem to invade their privacy, the absorption of
some Spanish Americans by Anglo-American churches and
their consequent loss of a specific listing as Spanish American Protestants. Add such conditions to the general deficiency of religious statistics, and the dearth of accurate
information on Spanish American Protestants becomes un-
derstandable.

Without adequate statistics, however, it is difficult to ap-
praise the success and failure of the Protestant approach to
Spanish Americans. But it is not the purpose of this study
to correct this deficiency. The materials necessary for an
accurate numerical description of Spanish American Protestants are simply not available, and neither this author nor
any other can write precisely about the numerical strength of

this part of Protestantism until the various denominations have done a more careful piece of homework in this area and have pooled their findings in such ways as to make possible a relatively accurate general enumeration of Spanish American Protestant church membership. We can only stress here the need for such information, without which churchmen who address themselves to the question of the Protestant impact upon Spanish Americans work in the dark.

. . . *Abandoned Fields*

The fragmentary figures that are available from denominational sources indicate that Protestants in general are ignorant of the appeal of Protestantism to Spanish-speaking people in the United States; unaware of the huge unchurched proportion of these people—neither Roman Catholic nor Protestant; uninformed of their socio-economic and spiritual needs; and indifferent both to Protestantism's obligation and its opportunity. The figures suggest that denominational officials know the problem and sense its challenge but are preoccupied by interests that are assumed to be more important. In a word, the figures leave with us the unmistakable conclusion that most Protestant churches are not taking the Spanish American challenge seriously.

The five and a half million Spanish Americans in the United States constitute not only the ethnic group with the largest number of unchurched people but also an ethnic group with a staggeringly high percentage of unchurched people. According to the *Yearbook of American Churches for 1963*, edited by Benson Y. Landis, church membership in the United States in 1961 was 63.4 per cent of the total population. Allowing the Roman Catholic Church an estimated 15 per cent of the Spanish American population in the United States, and the Protestant churches an estimated 5 per cent of these people as church members—both estimates are generous—there remains an estimated 80 per cent who have no church affiliation. In the nation at large, 63.4 per cent of the people are church members. (This figure does not include a large number of Protestant Sunday school members.) Among Spanish Americans, only 20 per cent—at the most—are church members. The challenge is plain: Spanish Americans make up the largest field in the United States for Protestant witness and service. How are the churches responding to that challenge and that opportunity?

.   .   .   *Selected Samples*

Such reports as are available from the mission agencies of the denominations are not encouraging and afford neither those denominations nor Protestantism at large any cause for complacency. Let us look, now, at some illustrative samples. There is no attempt here to be inclusive of all denominations or to cite all vital denominational programs among Spanish Americans. We are looking rather at a variety of reported approaches to a Spanish American ministry, none of which imply any smugness on the part of the responding denominations. On the contrary, the mood of each report was apologetic, confessing an inadequate interest on the part of Anglo-American Protestants in these denominations, bemoaning the lack of funds and workers, questioning the efficacy of techniques currently employed, and, in some cases, revealing the lack of a fundamental philosophy and strategy in the denominational approach to Spanish Americans. The reports reflect, also, the discouragement of denominational agencies confronted by the problems of paternalism and dependence in Spanish American mission churches that should now be growing into self-sufficiency and fraternalism. These samples of Spanish American activity are not offered here as bases for the comparison of the successes and failures of various churches, nor as complete statistical reports. They are reported solely for the particular insights that these selected illustrations give us into the Protestant approach to the Spanish American challenge, insights that can invigorate our response and give that response profitable direction.

One of the largest works among Spanish Americans is conducted by the Southern Baptist Convention under its department of language groups ministries. This denomination reports 580 missionaries (husbands and wives) working among Spanish Americans in the United States. Most of these missionaries are pastors of the 510 Spanish American congregations in the Southern Baptist Convention. These congregations are affiliated with local Baptist associations, state conventions, and the S.B.C. As would be expected from the large number of Baptists and the large number of Spanish Americans in Texas, New Mexico, Arizona, California, and Florida, the largest Spanish American work of this denomination is in these states. But with the geographical expansion of the Southern Baptist Convention, this church's Spanish American mission has been extended as far as the state of Washington in the Northwest and New York State in the East.

In most Spanish American churches in the S.B.C., the Sunday schools and other organizations dealing with young people are conducted in English and use English literature, but the preaching services are in Spanish. The number of churches using English for the sermons, with simultaneous translation into Spanish, is increasing. Although the Southern Baptists produce and use a great amount of Spanish-language literature, it appears that this church expects an early disappearance of Spanish-speaking churches as the younger, bilingual generation of Spanish Americans, disposed toward acculturation, replaces the older monolingual generation that has resisted absorption into Anglo-American culture. In line with this development, the S.B.C. reports a large and increasing number of Spanish Americans in the Anglo-American churches of the Southern Baptist Convention.

A similar large work among Spanish Americans is conducted by The Methodist Church. The 150 Spanish Methodist churches, like those of the Southern Baptist Convention, are concentrated most heavily in Texas (77), California (29), Arizona (15), and New Mexico (13). Twenty-five per cent of the 150 churches are self-supporting; the remainder are supported in varying degrees by The Methodist Church's division of national missions. The church edifices in which these congregations worship and study range from shacks to substantial buildings.

Although it is certainly not unmindful of the spiritual needs of Spanish Americans, The Methodist Church's Spanish American program is highly geared to the people's socio-economic needs. In the United States there are 14 Methodist clinics for Spanish Americans, directed toward the dual purpose of guarding the health of the people and educating them in diet and sanitary measures. In addition to these clinics, The Methodist Church owns and operates 31 Spanish American settlement houses that provide citizenship classes, religious services, day nurseries, Boy and Girl Scout troops, home economics and craft classes, pastoral counseling, and vocational guidance. Like the clinics, these settlement houses are heavily concentrated in Texas and California and minister mainly to Mexican Americans. The Methodist Church also provides four boarding schools, one home for girl students, and a special program for Spanish American theological students at the Perkins School of Theology, Dallas, Texas. Apparently, one of the show pieces of this denomination's Spanish American work is Lydia Patterson Institute in El Paso, Texas, which in 1962-1963 had 467 junior high and high school and other students engaged in a program to train Spanish American Methodist ministers, church workers, and laymen. Methodist sources report that this is the only educational institution in the United States given over solely to Spanish American youth.

This is obviously insufficient data for an analysis of the Methodist approach to Spanish Americans, and is not cited to imply that other denominations are less concerned about the physical and cultural needs. Several denominations have similar though less extensive programs. It is rather to show that this denomination sees service and witness as paralleling ministries and recognizes that service must sometimes precede witness. Christian charity is an end in itself and should not be used to gain the gospel a hearing. It flows toward the needy because they are needy and because the Christian is under Christ's orders to feed, heal, clothe, liberate, and teach, as well as under command to proclaim the salvation of all men in Christ. Even so, there can be no sincere proclamation of Jesus Christ that ignores the physical hungers, the mental poverty, and the personal agonies of men. Service and witness are identical twins; more correctly, they are Siamese twins: both die if either is separated from the other. The Methodist program, with its alternate strokes of witness and service, is illustrative of those Protestant approaches to Spanish Americans based on seeing and ministering to the whole man.

The Assemblies of God churches illustrate a third type of Protestant ministry to Spanish Americans. This denomination is the largest of the Pentecostal bodies in the United States: 8,233 churches and 508,602 members spread through every state in the Union. Ardently fundamentalist, literalist in scriptural view, given to speaking in tongues, this denomination has a zealous and effective Spanish American mission disproportionate to its size. Its churches in the United States produce, through their intense missionary emphasis, the same kind of success with Spanish Americans that is enjoyed by Pentecostal groups in Central and South America. The denomination has reported that in its Latin American district —west of the Ohio-Pennsylvania line—it has in its Spanish American ministry 634 ministers, 311 churches, and 2 Bible schools. In the Spanish-Eastern district (the Eastern states and Puerto Rico), the denomination has reported 219 ministers, 89 churches, and 2 Bible schools. All of its home Bible courses are being translated into Spanish, in addition to 10 Sunday school quarterlies and other papers that are already appearing in Spanish. The denomination's weekly, *The Pentecostal Evangel*, appears bimonthly in Spanish as *Poder*, meaning "Power." These Spanish-language materials are distributed to all Spanish-speaking Assemblies of God churches in the United States and Puerto Rico.

There is in the Pentecostal approach to Spanish Americans a primitive, sensual appeal that in its visual and audible aspects—though not in its basic concepts—is similar to the spiritualist and Indian religions that in the Caribbean and in Central and South America sometimes blend with Roman Catholicism and sometimes become a substitute for Roman Catholic pomp and mystery. Pentecostalism offers the unlearned, superstitious Spanish American a blending of the occult, the authoritative, and the physically demonstrable aspects of religion in simple and easily adopted form. It does not tax the mind, require formal education, nor raise the perplexing and often controversial social issues, but makes its claim to easily aroused and easily satisfied emotional and physical reactions. Consequently, for the uneducated Spanish American, the step from a hybrid Roman Catholic-Indian religion or from a spiritualist-animist faith to Pentecostalism is a short one. The success of Pentecostal missions to Spanish Americans, both here and abroad, is explained partly by this fact and partly by the laudable vigor, zeal, and self-sacrifice that, in general, characterize Pentecostal evangelism. Other Protestant denominations face a much more difficult task in winning the great masses of Spanish Americans and are attempting to accomplish this task with far less zeal and sacrifice. If this situation continues, it should not be surprising if the Pentecostalists and similar groups succeed where the older, better established Protestant denominations fail.

Several Protestant churches that have more limited Spanish American work are now lifting their sights and are preparing themselves, through thorough study, for a more extensive and effective Spanish American ministry. One example is the Protestant Episcopal Church. The home department of this denomination reports only 26 workers in the Spanish American field, 15 congregations, and 3,176 Spanish American members. But the Protestant Episcopal Church within recent years conducted two conferences from which came information and activities that are awakening and invigorating the Episcopal ministry to Spanish Americans.

The first of these conferences—both of which laid a sound foundation for a Spanish American ministry—occurred in January, 1959. Under the auspices of what was then this church's Division of Racial Minorities, a conference on Latin-American relations in the Southwest was held in Austin, Texas. Such experts on the Southwest's Spanish American culture as Carey McWilliams, Ralph Estrada, and George I. Sánchez were among the speakers who formulated recommendations for the improvement of the church's ministry to Spanish Americans in the Southwest.

The second conference was held under the same auspices in April, 1959, at the Cathedral of St. John the Divine in New York City. There the theme was the problems of Puerto Ricans in the United States. In this conference, too, such capable analysts as Joseph Monserrat, director of the New York office of the Migration Division, Department of Labor, Commonwealth of Puerto Rico, and a number of social workers and ministers with practical experience among Puerto Ricans prepared the church for a wide discussion "of the mission of the church, its strategy, its problems, and its future among Spanish-speaking fellow citizens." Summaries of these conferences were widely distributed. This is the kind of service that churches with limited Spanish American ministries can still perform for other churches as well as for themselves as they prepare for a wider Spanish American mission. Scholarly, yet compassionate, study of the problems and hopes of the Spanish American-Protestant confrontation is essential to progress in this field.

The Presbyterian Church, U.S., is an illustration of those churches that are unhappy about their ministry to Spanish Americans, that are developing an uneasy conscience about their neglect of these people, and that are experiencing an awakening concern about and devotion to their Spanish American ministry. It would be unkind to let this church confess its failures in public if we did not see in this confession the creative mood to which most Protestant churches have to be summoned.

In the Synod of Texas, there are only 38 Presbyterian Spanish churches with a membership of 3,082. These facts compelled this church to say of itself, "It will be observed immediately that the Presbyterian Church, U.S., is making a barely discernible scratch on the surface of the needs of the people for the gospel." In the state of Texas, in which the Spanish American population increased 131 per cent in a 17-year period and the membership of the Spanish American Presbyterian churches increased only 3 per cent, it behooves the Presbyterian Church, U.S., to raise, as it is doing, critical, searching questions about its ministry to Spanish Americans. In 1960, the Presbyterian Church, U.S., had only one Spanish American preministerial student in training— and that one the only potential ministerial candidate for the next six years. Sixty-eight per cent of its ordained Spanish American ministers were at that time in the forty to fifty-nine year age range, and 16 per cent of the ordained ministers were over sixty years of age. Reports also indicated a severe shortage of Presbyterian literature in Spanish.

These are not easy confessions for an otherwise successful

denomination to make. But the confession is significant; it is an encouraging sign of the church's awakening to a neglected duty and its developing awareness that unchurched Spanish Americans are its responsibility. There are churches whose ministries to Spanish Americans suffer deficiencies similar to the self-confessed failures of the Presbyterian Church, U.S., but that are not yet gripped by a vision of what all the churches must do to meet the whole need of the most unchurched minority in the United States. Ignorance, indifference, neglect—this has been the tragic history of the Anglo-Protestant approach to Spanish Americans. The new day and the new challenge demand of Protestant churches responsible programs of education, service, and fraternity.

Increasingly, the bulletin boards and newspaper advertisements of local Anglo-American Protestant churches carry the words: "*Se habla español*," a tacit invitation to the Spanish-speaking people of the neighborhood. Some of these Anglo-American churches go further, issuing specific invitations to Spanish Americans in Spanish-language newspapers, or announcing services in Spanish on the Saturday church page of English-language papers. For example, *La Prensa* for Sunday, February 17, 1963, carried an advertisement that listed services in Spanish and in English at The Methodist Church's Broadway Temple and that gave the name of the Spanish American as well as the Anglo-American minister.

The same issue of *La Prensa* featured an article in Spanish by Lydia Ellorin, which gave a full description of the varied programs that The Riverside Church offers to Spanish-speaking people. This description not only invited Spanish Americans to the Spanish-language services in the church's Christ Chapel, to classes for new members, to courses in the arts and trades for the neighborhood, and to Bible study classes, but also welcomed all people to the English-language programs and worship services. Miss Ellorin wrote: "In The

Riverside Church there is a magnificent opportunity for those people who want to become integrated into the community in which they reside and adapt themselves to the plane of the society in which they live."

These two churches are cited solely as illustrations and with full awareness that there are other Anglo-American churches in New York City, Chicago, Miami, Los Angeles, and elsewhere that are doing a similar and comparable work. And there are many smaller Anglo-American churches that, with more limited resources, facilities, and opportunities, are making a commendable effort to serve the socio-economic and spiritual needs of Spanish Americans in their communities. There is no way to measure the extent and the effectiveness of these programs, but it can be said that as Spanish Americans are more widely dispersed in the general society, the local church, as it has opportunity, must assume increasing responsibility for the ministry to Spanish Americans.

. . .   *The United Approach*

In addition to ignorance, indifference, and neglect, there is another tragedy that could blight the Protestant ministry to Spanish Americans—and that is a rigidly unilateral denominational approach. The purpose of the ministry to Spanish Americans is not to make Baptists, Methodists, Presbyterians, or Episcopalians of them but to win them to voluntary professions of faith in Jesus Christ and to make available to them the love and the helpfulness of their more fortunate fellow Christians. The goal is to win them to Jesus Christ, not to a denominational identification. Therefore, we should now note examples of the cooperative Protestant ministry to Spanish Americans.

Surely one of the best known and probably one of the most effective united ministries to Spanish Americans is the East Harlem Protestant Parish. Located at 306 East 103rd Street, New York City, in one of the most congested, racially heterogeneous, low-income, crime-infested slums in the United States, this interdenominational parish ministers to an increasing number of the Puerto Ricans who are flooding an already over-populated East Harlem. As Paul R. Carlson, associate director of the office of information of the United Presbyterian Church in the U.S.A., put it, in East Harlem "close to a quarter million people look upon this square-mile of projects, of ramshackle tenements, and fetid pavements as their home." Here, where Park Avenue wealth and harsh Harlem poverty are side by side in sharp contrast, human dignity and personality are crushed. Here are the graphic examples of inadequate housing, racial discrimination, juvenile crime, dilapidated and overcrowded schools, shattered family life, unemployment—all of the major social, economic, and moral evils in the United States in their most acute, virulent, and contagious form. Yet, until 1948, the desperate and despairing people of this area were ignored by the major Protestant denominations.

In that year, two Union Seminary graduates conducted the first worship service of the East Harlem Protestant Parish in a storefront church, having as their entire congregation one elderly Puerto Rican woman. Eventually, the ministers and their church won the confidence of the neighborhood. Supported by six of the major Protestant denominations (American Baptist, Evangelical United Brethren, Methodist, United Presbyterian, Reformed, and United Church), the parish now conducts an interdenominational "group ministry" from three church centers within a six-block area. Soon a new $220,000 center, the Church of the Resurrection, will be built. The parish provides a medical and mental health center, social service, and Christian education programs, in addition to an intensive program of rehabilitation for narcotics addicts.

Interdenominational support secures for the East Harlem Protestant Parish freedom to break with traditional church patterns and to venture into new ways of handling the extraordinary human problems in East Harlem. The ecumenical character of the parish also encourages innovation in the production of new and varied patterns of worship that appeal to and satisfy the heterogeneous religions, traditions, and spiritual needs in the community. Here, in a neighborhood that is a polyglot mixture of peoples, where Puerto Ricans predominate, with American Negroes a close second, Protestants in mutual dedication have created what the parish calls "a family of God, gathered together for worship, study, fellowship, and prayer, and then sent forth on his mission of service and witness in the world." This is an Exhibit A of what Protestant cooperation can do in a mutual ministry to Spanish Americans trapped in the ghettos of our great cities.

The East Harlem Protestant Parish is both the glory and the shame of the Protestant ministry to Spanish Americans —the glory, in its remarkably successful fifteen-year-old history; the shame, in that it reminds us of what can be and is not being done for Spanish Americans in the inner cities of our great metropolitan areas. The parish is not unique; the New York City Mission Society's Church of the Good Neighbor in East Harlem, for example, has a similar program. But the scarcity of such projects, the withdrawal of many Anglo-American churches from the congested heartlands of the urban complexes to the secluded suburbs, their failure to leave behind them a witness to the gospel and a ministry to the people, and sometimes their heroic but shortsighted determination to "go it alone" with a strictly denominational witness—these are the failures that the successes of the East Harlem Protestant Parish dramatize. The problem and the opportunity of the ministry to Spanish Americans will not have been fully engaged by the resources and the dedication of the Protestant churches until such projects as the East Harlem Protestant Parish are commonplace rather than exceptional.

In addition to the missions to Spanish Americans provided by denominations working alone and together, and the work of local churches—both Spanish and Anglo-American —the ministries of local and state councils of churches and the Division of Home Missions of the National Council of the Churches of Christ in the United States of America should be cited. In no area is this work more impressive than in the forty-four-year-old Migrant Ministry under the guidance and supervision of the Division of Home Missions of the National Council. This work, originated by missionary minded women who, in 1920, saw the need for such witness and service among migrant Negroes in New Jersey, grew, spread, and was adopted by the Home Missions Council of North America. In 1950, the Home Missions Council became part of the Division of Home Missions of the newly formed National Council of Churches, and a National Migrant Committee was organized to promote and supervise this specialized ministry.

This national committee adopted the following Statement of Purpose in 1953:

In the Migrant Ministry the churches are united to serve men, women, and children who are following the crops. This program is centered in the Christian faith and seeks to share that faith with the migrant, and to develop in him a sense of his personal worth, belonging, and responsibility. It seeks to awaken the community to the opportunity and obligation of sharing equally all the protective benefits and warmth of community life. It challenges the local churches to include these seasonal neighbors in their concern and full fellowship. It calls on the state and nation to apply Christian principles to the economy in which migrants live and work.

This stated purpose is quoted in full to show the four-directional movement essential to a migrant ministry but essential also to most Christian approaches to Spanish Americans: toward the migrant, the community, the local churches, and the state and national governments. No council would claim that this goal is being accomplished. It defines, nevertheless, the aims that should be held in the sights of all ministries to Spanish Americans.

Most churches have recognized, as did those in the Michigan Council, "that this ministry is too big for them to do alone, that there are needs of the migrant which cannot be separated from the religious needs if the churches are to follow the example of Jesus in his ministry." The symbol of the Migrant Ministry—the nation, the cross, and the people encircled by the words "The Churches Working Together" —expresses the ideal Protestant witness and service to Spanish Americans. Churches are also discovering, through the Migrant Ministry, that the mission to Spanish Americans, migrant or otherwise, must not be partial but must be addressed to the whole man. There is no substitute for an ecumenical ministry to the total need of Spanish Americans.

Increasingly during the past forty-four years the ecumenical ministry to migrants has become a ministry to Spanish Americans. In 1960, in Michigan, for example, there were 71,785 total out-of-state workers in the seasonal groups. Of this number, 11,500 were Mexican Nationals (citizens of Mexico, mostly males) and 32,000 were from Texas, most of them being Mexican Americans. In Wisconsin, in the same year, the great majority of migrants were Spanish speaking. The continuing flow of Mexicans into the United States and the increasing immigration of Puerto Ricans accelerates this trend. The ministry to Spanish Americans can therefore never be accomplished outside of an intensified mission to migrant workers.

What is the scope and nature of this united Protestant ministry to Spanish American migrants? In a listing of national organizations for migrant farm workers and their families compiled by the United States Department of Labor, the Division of Home Missions of the National Council of

Churches announces the following programs: integration of migratory workers with the community where they are temporarily located; Sunday schools, vacation church schools, weekday religious education, and worship services all geared to the background, needs, and understanding of the people; service to infants and young children needing special care and protection: child care centers, well baby clinics, health services; activities for school age children and summer schools to supplement interrupted education; fellowship, recreation, and prevocational training and guidance; family night activities, both recreational and educational; counseling; interpretation of the needs of the people and the Migrant Ministry through speeches, radio, newspapers, television, etc.; enlistment of the services of local, state, and national agencies. In its promotion material, the Wisconsin Council of Churches reduces these theoretical purposes to their human terms:

Extending a loving hand, providing food where there is none, taking the ill to a doctor or hospital, helping to meet a financial problem, or sitting on a cherry or cucumber box in a humble home just listening with a sympathetic ear to their troubles, holding parental clinics, taking clothes and shoes to families in need, providing layettes for babies, helping to provide Rebecca with much-needed glasses. . . . Julia on a broken bed in a cramped little cabin, moaning in pain. . . . Roberto suffering an aching tooth. . . . José and Juanita, who had lost their first baby. . . . Migrants are people without any church home and children without schooling, without permanent homes and steady work.

Bringing Christ and the charities of Christ to such people —this is the Migrant Ministry.

Despite occasional instances of success in the denominational, local, and ecumenical approach to Spanish Americans, it must be admitted that the record thus far is bleak. By whatever measurement we use—membership, converts, churches, clinics, literature, or what not—the Protestant ministry to Spanish Americans has suffered from the lack of vision, concern, dedication, workers, and financial resources. It remains the most exciting and promising frontier confronting the Protestant churches in the United States today. Such successes as have been achieved challenge and encourage the Protestant churches to move toward the masses of unchurched Spanish Americans in the United States in a well planned, massive program of Christian witness and service.

৩ 7 WHAT THE CHURCHES SHOULD DO

. . .   *Challenge and Opportunity*

When we ask what Protestant churches should do, we are handicapped in answering by the fact that thus far the Protestant ministry to Spanish Americans leaves us little history to build on. Take two examples: evangelical missionary work among Spanish-speaking people in New Mexico began, according to Presbyterian claims, in a mission school in Santa Fe in 1867, preceded only by haphazard Baptist, Presbyterian, and Methodist missions in 1849 and 1850. But in the nearly one hundred years of organized evangelical ministry to the indigenous people of New Mexico and to their kinsmen who have in that time come north from Mexico, Protestants have not by any measurement made disciples in numbers that merit the term "successful." No value can be put on any life won to Jesus Christ, nor are business world standards of success and failure, profit and loss applicable to Christian missions. For it may be true, as Dwight L. Moody, the great evangelist, put it, that to convert a child is to convert a multiplication table. Nevertheless,

Protestants are under orders to "Go therefore and make disciples of all nations, baptizing them in the name of the Father and of the Son and of the Holy Spirit, teaching them to observe all that I have commanded you; and lo, I am with you always, to the close of the age." While obeying the command elsewhere, Protestants neglected to obey it in New Mexico.

In neighboring Texas, with a longer history of Protestant influence, there are now only 708 Spanish American Protestant churches with a total of 41,000 members out of the roughly one and a half million Spanish Americans in that state. Thus, approximately 1,460,000 Spanish Americans in Texas are not reached for Christ through Protestant churches. If 20 per cent of Texas Spanish Americans are reached by the Roman Catholic Church, then more than a million are not touched by the witness or service of any Christian church. Admittedly, these are loose approximations. They do not include the small number of Spanish Americans who attend Anglo-American churches or the children of most Spanish American Protestants. Even so, in a state in which the Spanish American population increased by 131 per cent from 1940 to 1957, these are not figures over which Protestants can rejoice nor in which they can take pride. It is apparent from these two examples that Protestant churches have not "gone" to Spanish Americans in the full sense of the grand commission. Our failures prove that our "going" to these people has been for most of its history halfhearted and poorly prepared, lacking in understanding and insight, and has come alive only in recent years to the need, the challenge, and the opportunity of a Protestant ministry to Spanish Americans.

If we learn from our successes, meager as they have been, the next hundred years can be the golden century of the Protestant-Spanish American encounter. It can be a century in which millions rather than thousands of Spanish Americans in the United States will say to Protestantism's invitation, "*This* is my religion. This is what I have been looking for." It can be a century in which Anglo-Protestantism, surfeited with material successes and increasingly identified with American culture, receives from the Spanish American community the spirit, the insight, and the discipline needed for revival. There is a key that has turned in the minds and hearts of a few Protestants and must turn in hundreds of thousands of such hearts and minds if the vision of a golden century is to become a reality. That key is the conviction that Spanish Americans *are* an area of Protestant concern. They cannot be left to the care of the church that, for so many centuries, dominated their culture and neglected their moral and spiritual welfare, even though that church, like some Protestant churches, shows an awakening interest in Spanish Americans. The combined efforts and resources of Protestants and Roman Catholics, spent at the highest possible level, would not be enough for the need. Spanish Americans are people; most of them are needy people. Needy people are Protestantism's concern. The faster this key turns in Protestant minds and hearts—especially on the local level, more especially in local churches in areas where Spanish Americans are concentrated—the sooner will begin the golden century.

. . .   *Lessons from Trial and Error*

In one long paragraph in which he cites Beatrice Griffith[1] as the source of some of his material, John H. Burma gives a fairly complete explanation of Protestantism's successes and failures among Spanish Americans:

Protestant churches have made considerably larger numbers of converts among Mexican Americans in the United States than

---

[1] Griffith, Beatrice. *American Me.* Boston: Houghton Mifflin Co., 1948.

among residents in Mexico; the percentage, although small, is probably five times as great as in Mexico. The three major reasons for this change in religious allegiance seem to be: (1) active proselytizing by various Protestant churches; (2) social welfare services, settlement houses, recreation programs and other extra-ecclesiastical activities of Protestant groups; (3) the general assimilative process at work on second- and third-generation young people. That the number changing to Protestantism is not greater is probably due to weaknesses on the part of some churches; Mexican Protestant churches are usually of the mission type, small, and rarely self-supporting; frequently they do a poor public relations job, do not make full use of musical possibilities, and seriously lack physical attractiveness. Protestant settlement houses do not make a wide impression, but they fill an important place in the growth of many Mexican-American leaders whom they help with encouragement, imparting American outlook and industry and providing scholarships.[2]

This is a good summary statement, but it needs one correction and several additions. Burma accepts the common and erroneous assumption—or so implies—that a Spanish American who becomes a Protestant is necessarily a convert from Catholicism. We have seen that this is not so. Although many Mexican American Protestants were formerly Roman Catholics, or nominally so, many of them, like Protestant Cubans and Puerto Ricans, were originally unchurched. In addition to this correction, we must add to Burma's list one major reason for the Protestant churches' success and one major reason for their failure. The picture is not complete and the guidance it can give us is misleading without these additions.

With the aid of Griffith and Burma we have listed three major reasons why Spanish Americans become Protestants. The fourth reason is the impact of individual Protestants

---

[2] Burma, John H. *Spanish-Speaking Groups in the United States*, p. 83. Durham: Duke University Press, 1954.

and Protestant families who live genuinely devout Christian lives in the presence of Spanish Americans who have known only a pompous, vapid brand of Roman Catholicism. There is no more graphic story of this kind of witness than that of Alfonso Rodriguez Hidalgo, first president of the union seminary, Seminario Evangélico de Teología, Matanzas, Cuba, until the Communist-controlled Castro regime made life unbearable for him and his family on the island, and now associate director of the Departmento Hispano Americano of the Board of National Missions of the United Presbyterian Church. When Rodriguez was fourteen years old, he came to a Memphis, Tennessee, hospital for a series of emotionally and physically taxing surgical treatments. After a period of treatments, the hospital doctors recommended a change of environment for the boy. A Christian family invited him to be a guest in their home. For five consecutive summers he lived in that home. Let him complete the story: "By the grace of God and also by the life of those Christian people (no one proselyted; no one approached me), my mother and I and every one of my five brothers changed from the Roman Catholic to the Protestant church. This was the Christian faith we had been longing for."

No one keeps statistics on this kind of conversion to Protestantism, and Protestantism is reluctant to make capital of the number of Roman Catholics who become Protestants. But this is what one Christian family can do through the faithful practice of its Christianity. The winning of Alfonso Rodriguez by Christian example—to say nothing of the winning of his mother and brothers—was, in Moody's phrase, the converting of a multiplication table.

But if, on the one hand, devout Christian families can win Spanish Americans by a witness of Christian deeds, on the other hand, families who wear the name of Christ but do not practice his nondiscriminative love can alienate Spanish Americans from all Christianity permanently. So to the list of reasons for the failure of Protestants to win Spanish Americans we must add the racial prejudice and social snobbery that many Christians—Protestants and Roman Catholics—exhibit toward Spanish Americans. We have seen that the darkest skinned Mexican Americans and, of course, the Cuban and Puerto Rican Negroes, share the crippling and humiliating discriminations that white America heaps upon black America. And most Spanish Americans, whatever their hue and even though they are technically classified as white, experience degrading rejection because of their racial visibility. We have already noted the scope of this discrimination against Spanish-speaking people in American society and have explored the depths of the psychic and societal wounds it inflicts. We note now that when this prejudice is practiced by Christian people, it seriously hampers Christian activity among Spanish American people.

Beatrice Griffith rightly identified this problem as one of the most serious and successful blocks to Protestant missions:

Like Catholicism, organized Protestantism has not taken a definite stand either on the Negro or the Mexican in America. A few church leaders have made their convictions clear by their actions, but their very struggles demonstrate that the Church hasn't done the job it could do, either in sufficiently backing young men and women leaders, or in aligning itself with progressive movements to break down prejudice and discrimination.

The elaborate alibis and pretexts of Protestant churchgoers to avoid responsibility toward the Mexicans take these forms: "They are Catholics and not our concern. They are a subnormal race, mostly Indian; they can't learn our American way of living and don't want to; they are just greasers and could never be anything anyway. The crimes of this town come from these people—we're already paying out more for their health and charity than for any group. They cause all the trouble in our community." [3]

─────────────
[3] Griffith, op. cit., pp. 190-191.

Undoubtedly, many twisted feelings and distorted thoughts lie behind such descriptions of Spanish Americans, but all of them are typical of the clichés and generalities used by racists to justify prejudice and discrimination. We can hardly expect Spanish Americans who hear themselves so described by Anglo-Americans to respond gratefully to the invitation of Anglo-American churches.

In this day when the whole nation is more attuned to and concerned about the problems of racial and religious plural-ism than ever before, the rejection of the Spanish American as "different" and as unacceptable lessens slightly and takes on more genteel and subtle forms. In restaurants, barber shops, hotels, for example, the old and openly exclusive sign "No Mexicans Allowed" now reads, "We Reserve the Right to Serve," a cunning emendation that gets the point across just as unmistakably and just as offensively. In churches, of course, there are no such signs. But a church people who resent the presence of Spanish Americans have an amazing ingenuity in conveying that feeling to the unwanted visitors. In fact, where the rejection of Spanish Americans is strongly felt by Anglo-American Christians, it cannot be concealed from a sensitive people who have known and experienced that rejection in all its crass and subtle expressions.

It is not enough for the Anglo-American Protestant church to establish and support Spanish-speaking missions for Span-ish Americans or settlement houses that are isolated from the Anglo-American church community. Such services are essential to the total Protestant ministry to Spanish Ameri-cans—as we shall see. But unless they are geared into a total program that receives Spanish Americans fully into the whole Christian community, they will, in the end, blight rather than bless the Protestant mission. The isolated, paternalistic mission will be interpreted by Spanish Americans—and usually rightly so—as the white man's most cunning and most despicable rejection of his Spanish American neighbor.

Put bluntly, such missions will be resented as the Anglo-American Christian's strategy for rejection of the Spanish American Christian: "give him a church of his own and perhaps he will not seek admission to ours."

Likewise, the social welfare services that are remotely administered by Anglo-Americans and stop far short of genuine Christian fellowship will be viewed by alert Spanish Americans as the Anglo-American's effort to solve a sociological dilemma rather than an effort to establish with the Spanish American a true Christian identity. Missions, Spanish-speaking churches, welfare programs—all three are indispensable to the Protestant ministry to Spanish Americans. But unless such programs assume and serve inclusive Christian community as one of their primary and essential goals, unless they genuinely desire and actively seek Spanish Americans as unqualified members of the Christian family, they may do great harm in one area while they are doing good in another. Witness and service that do not produce unity may still have some value, but the value is not a Christian one. Witness and service that disrupt or prevent or postpone Christian unity are neither a Christian witness nor a Christian service. The Christian objective is all three—witness, service, and unity—in such interpenetration that there is no discerning where the one ends and the other begins. A Protestant ministry to Spanish Americans that has this total objective as its official policy, and in which official policy is not refuted by local practice, will succeed. Where there is no such guiding design, the ministry to Spanish Americans will fail.

We noted in Chapter 3 that as a minor ethnic group in the United States, Spanish Americans have six primary needs: acceptance, organization, leadership, education, health, and the gospel. We discovered in Chapter 4 that though there are no unique Spanish American distinctions, there are certain predominant Spanish American traits that have been called out by a shared cultural inheritance, a particular environment, and a distinct history. The failure of the Protestant ministry to Spanish Americans can be divided into two parts; the inadequacy of the Protestant mission itself; and the refusal of the mission to direct and adapt itself to the needs and to the predominant traits of Spanish Americans. The success of the Protestant ministry to Spanish-speaking people, on the other hand, occurs only when that ministry is virile, selflessly devoted to the gospel and to the people, adequately supported by talent and resources, and deliberately shaped to the demonstrated needs and the prevailing traits of the people. From these facts emerges the pattern of a successful ministry to Spanish Americans.

We shall examine this pattern in some detail, but in a preliminary statement we can say that such a ministry must be deeply concerned about and unreservedly and actively dedicated to Spanish American people in the spirit and through the power of Christ. It must be a total response to their need for Christian witness, service, and unity. It must take account of those cultural and personal characteristics that are more pronounced in Spanish than they are in Anglo-Americans. It must be a ministry that seeks not only the winning of Spanish Americans but that knows that the greatly needed reformation of the Protestant churches in the United States can come by way of an evangelical Spanish American witness and service in unity with Anglo-American Protestants. These are the rough boundaries of a successful ministry to Spanish Americans. Let us walk leisurely back and forth across this bounded area and see what we find.

.   .   .   *Guidelines: The Individual*

Let us begin our pattern for a mission to Spanish Americans with a startling, extravagant statement that seems to contradict everything said thus far: There is no such thing as a ministry to Spanish Americans. Let us examine this exaggeration. God calls a people to repentance and return, to judgment and mercy, to punishment and love. But however collective his call, he expects it to be heard and responded to by persons, one by one. His act of redeeming love in Jesus Christ is for all people, but it must be accepted by each person for himself, if at all. The Christian proclamation of that act must be to all people but, again, can be responded to only by each person individually and for himself. In this sense, the ministry we are discussing is not to a mass of indistinguishably homogeneous people called Spanish Americans but, rather, to needful individuals who happen to share certain ethnic identities with other people and among those people find their strongest bonds of association and kinship. In this sense, then, there is no Christian ministry to Spanish Americans; there is only a ministry to individual Spanish Americans. Our concern is for all, but it pales if it does not focus on the one.

This may seem a fine and needless distinction, but if we permit it to stand for a time, it will help us to see one of the deadliest snares fashioned by collective titles, even the best of such titles. The peril is that the collective phrases obscure the individual, submerging his hopes and fears, his agonies and joys in the depersonalized mass. Derogatory names for Spanish-speaking people have the destruction of the individual as their specific purpose, but official and accepted population titles can have the same disastrous effect: the obliteration of the individual. We can think or speak rather casually of the physical, social, and spiritual needs of Spanish Americans. No sensitive response is demanded by such academics. But it is something quite different to be confronted personally by Juan Gonzales, a migrant worker whose tuberculosis now robs his family of their only support; by María Hernández, whose common-law husband has abandoned her and their children; by Ricardo Quiroga, keen and inquisitive ten-year-old who hopes to go to college some day; by Miguel Medina, who walks alone and uninvited into a settlement house he had previously stoned and takes the first step toward a Christian life; by Dr. Elivd Garcia Treviño, accomplished physician of chronic diseases and geriatrics, who with his large family serves Christ in a prominent Baptist church. With the exception of the last, these names are fictitious, but the people they represent are real. What must be borne in mind is the fact that the Protestant mission is not a mass appeal to a population blob called Spanish Americans but to individuals whom it can help and by whom it can be helped: Juan, María, Ricardo, Miguel, Dr. Garcia. "Personalize your sympathies," said the late Dean William Inge of St. Paul's Cathedral, London, "depersonalize your antipathies." It is a good rule for the mission about which we are here concerned. Spanish Americans are our "sympathies"; affection, concern, and gratitude require that we personalize them, thinking not of an ethnic group, a social segment, but of individuals, persons whose strengths and weaknesses, resources and deficiencies—in other words, whose elemental humanness—claim us in Christ.

So we are thinking in terms of the individual and we have noted in Chapter 4 that this individual has a keen awareness of and an intense regard for his individuality. The trait is universal; its intensity is typically Spanish American. What the Spanish American calls *dignidad*—respect for the dignity of the person—is in him so prominent and suffuses so much of his life that the universal trait becomes in him a distinctive characteristic. It influences his attitude toward work, time, schedule, education, government, the church, and other people. The individualism of the Anglo-American does not reach the same extremes. The Anglo-American, for example, will teach his children a wholly new system of mathematics —which he is now doing—because the production and operation of intricate computers requires such a mathematics. The Spanish American is likely to resist an education that subjects his individuality to a machine and that adapts him to civilization rather than adapting civilization to him. The church that ignores this stress upon individualism and personal dignity in its very deepest sense is not likely to have a long success in dealing with Spanish Americans.

Mrs. Matilde Peréz de Silva, coordinator of Social Services, Migration Division, Department of Labor, Commonwealth of Puerto Rico, tells us how knowledge of this psychological fact must be applied to the practical situation:

We have general rules which help us to be more or less successful with them:

First, we have great respect for the individual. This sense of *dignidad* (personal dignity) we never overlook and we protect this feeling as a source of personal strength. We treat everybody with the same deference, whether they are very high society or very uneducated people. Secondly, we always try to remember that it is *their problem* and necessarily they are involved in it. . . . Never forget that it is their problem and they will want to manage the situation their own way according to *their* experience in Puerto Rico, although the same approach may not be possible here. . . . They have a terrific capacity for *aguante* (strength) and can put up with great hardships if they are set in accomplishing something. They have stamina (sometimes under the appearance of dullness) and that is something that should not be destroyed by over-direction or under-estimation of their capacity to function adequately. We have to give them support all along to give them security. You will be surprised how many times they find a satisfactory solution that you would never have dreamed of.[4]

If we apply these several closely related and interlarded suggestions to the ministry to Spanish Americans, we see the need to transform that ministry from a paternalistic to a fraternal basis as rapidly as possible. To assume that the

---

[4] *Summary of Conference on Problems of Puerto Ricans in the United States,* p. 32. Home Department, The National Council of the Protestant Episcopal Church, 1962.

Protestant ministry to Spanish Americans is something
Anglo-Americans do for Spanish-speaking people is to accept
an archaic, false, and offensive view of the Christian mission.
Yet this is what too frequently happens. A Spanish American
minister in the Southwest said in an interview: "No one
ever asks us what we think." It was his way of claiming the
problem and offering to bring to it unused insights and
strengths. This does not mean that Anglo-Americans should
say to Spanish Americans: "It's your problem; you take care
of it." Most Spanish-speaking churches are not ready for
complete independence. It means, rather, that Spanish and
Anglo-American Christians should say to each other: "These
are *our* problems; let us work them out together." Spanish
Americans, in a word, resent being an object, even an object
of charity. The more they participate, the more they are involved at all levels of responsibility and authority, the more
effective the ministry will be. In Cuba, the Lower Rio
Grande Valley, and Puerto Rico, Spanish American Protestants have shown extraordinary ability in managing their
own affairs. Considering the brevity of the time Protestantism
has been in these areas, the success of the churches in assuming responsibility for the organization, administration, support, and promotion of their affairs has been extraordinary.
This is the result of a let's-do-it-together policy on the part
of missionaries and local Protestants. No policy will work as
well as this one in Spanish American Protestantism.

Spanish American respect for the dignity of the person
requires not only that Protestant missions be cooperatively
rather than paternally developed, but also that Spanish
Americans who venture into Anglo-American churches be
neither rebuffed by cold disregard nor embarrassed by a
patronizing and overly solicitous welcome. They should be
received with gracious hospitality, not with an attention that
makes them feel that they are objects of curiosity. Spanish-
speaking people have in their own language a vocabulary of

intimacy that is used only by family members and close friends. It is insulting to be addressed in those terms by strangers. There is little danger that Anglo-Americans will use the wrong Spanish vocabulary in welcoming Spanish Americans to their churches. But there is a danger that the Anglo-American will employ in his greeting an offensive air of familiarity and will embarrass the visitors rather than put them at ease. It will be a fortunate day for Protestant churches when their racial, social, and ethnic sameness is so shattered that the appearance of an Oriental, a Negro, or a Spanish American in a predominantly Anglo-American Protestant church is an occasion to welcome another human being to Christ's fold rather than an event that taxes the church's ability to make the exceptional person feel at home.

Respect for the dignity of the person—what an opening this is for the Christian gospel in Protestant terms! A people who have this kind of sensitivity to personality are ripe for the Reformation that removed the church from and restored the individual to the center of religious concern. A Reformation theology and a Reformation ethic—highlighting the inestimable value of the individual in the sight of God, freeing man from the monstrous institutions that, created by him, became his master—speak to the spirit of the Spanish American. This is not all but is certainly a large part of the appeal of Protestantism to the Spanish American. When the Spanish American, newly come to Protestantism, says: "This is the religion I have been looking for," he expresses gratitude in part for a religion that tramples institutions and gives the individual his self-respect as a child of God.

· · ·   *The Church and the*
Socio-economic Needs

The Spanish American's extraordinary sense of personal dignity is offended by his status in American society. He is close to the bottom of the nation's socio-economic totem

pole. In education, health, employment, and housing he
occupies the lowest stratum. This is not what he wants or
deserves; it is not the best of which he is capable; but there
he is. At that level he is not making his finest contribution
to the commonwealth. He needs help. The help he receives
will be repaid in the good it does him and in multiplied
benefits to the nation. The church that protests its concern
for this man as a living soul but ignores the oppressive social
conditions under which he lives is false to the gospel and to
the man. The Protestant churches have been at their best
where they have seen this need and have responded to it,
making their response an end in itself rather than a means
to convert non-Protestant Spanish Americans. Such programs
as have already been cited—settlement houses, schools, welfare activities in interdenominational, inner city parishes,
varied programs for migrants—should be intensified to the
full extent of the resources of the churches.

The response of the churches to the plight of Cuban
refugees in Florida is exemplary. More than thirty com-
munions working through Church World Service in cooperation with local and national government have performed a
variety of services to meet the needs of the escapees from
the Fidel Castro government: spiritual guidance, English
classes, distribution of clothing, counseling, housing, sup-
plemental feeding, and resettlement in other parts of the
United States. In any given month an estimated five to
seven thousand refugees receive assistance through the various Protestant centers established in Dade County for this
purpose. This is a "crash" program established to meet a
crisis. The extent of that crisis, the needs that it raises, and
the services of the churches should not be underestimated.

Yet, though it is more dramatic, it is not more serious or
demanding than two other situations that have been with
us all along and about which, comparably, the churches have
done little: the problem of the migrant Spanish American

—one of the most serious social problems in the United States—and the problem of Spanish Americans in the ghettos of our great cities. Greater Miami is second only to Havana in the number of Cubans. But for a much longer time, more Mexicans have lived in Los Angeles, California, than in any other city in the world except Mexico City, and New York City has for some time had more Puerto Ricans than any city in Puerto Rico. And the Spanish Americans in these cities, as we know, live lives of desperation under the most deplorable conditions. These situations, and similar ones in other cities of the Southwest, deserve local and national "crash" programs at the interdenominational level. The problem is too big for the haphazard, hit-or-miss activities of local churches and denominations working unilaterally. These local churches should do what they can for individual families, but the big problem will be solved only by collective action.

Protestant responsibility for the social welfare of Spanish Americans is not discharged when the churches do all that they can do. There are areas of distress and oppression that are too big for the church and that only the action of local, state, and national governments can correct. Here it is the role of the churches, doing what they can, to press for legislation that will make possible changes in the status of those Spanish Americans who live at a substandard level in the midst of American affluence. One does not have to search long to find those areas in which government action is called for.

Government aid is needed to speed the dispersal of Puerto Ricans over a wider area and reduce their concentration in metropolitan New York; to lift the wage level of migrants; to tighten enforcement of compulsory school attendance laws; to open housing areas restricted to Spanish Americans (there are 60,000 Mexican Americans living in the west side slum of San Antonio, Texas, prisoners of restricted housing);

to provide adequate health services and training in personal hygiene and sanitation for poverty-stricken Mexican Americans along the border; to condemn vermin-infested, fetid, dilapidated tenements in which thousands of Puerto Ricans are housed. The need is extensive; the resistance to such legislation is great; the voice of the church, if united and sufficiently vocal, could be decisive. It is futile for the church to provide various remedial services through settlement houses, adult classes, health clinics, and all its other rescue operations if at the same time it fails to engage governments and other agencies in preventive actions that make the remedial programs unnecessary. Prevention is as much the role of the church as is correction.

. . .   *The Church as Interpreter*

The highly individualistic, intensely self-respecting and self-conscious Spanish American, living his life under crushing social conditions, lives also a life in triple suspension: between two cultures, between two generations, between two localities. First, as we noted, he is marginal to two cultures: the inherited Spanish American and the aggressive, overwhelming Anglo-American culture. He is in tension between the two—unwilling to desert the old, reluctant to repudiate the new. There is much that is precious to him in his tradition, much that is appealing to him in the Anglo-American world. Somehow he must maintain his grasp upon both, and the effort is often exhausting.

Second, if he is middle-aged or older, he is marginal to two generations—that of his parents and that of his children. Young people adapt quickly to any new environment to which they are exposed; older people find adaptation much more difficult. Conflict between the older-generation Spanish American, rooted in the past, and the younger generation, looking toward the future, creates intolerable problems for both. This is especially true where the environment encourages young people to rebel against their elders; family life is destroyed and the young people, bereft of this authority and insufficiently supervised by law-enforcement agencies, drift into delinquency. The gang displaces the family as authority and as social cosmos.

Third, if he is an average Spanish American, he is not only midway between cultures and generations but is also in physical transition. He is a Cuban, newly arrived from the island; a Puerto Rican fresh from San Juan or journeying back and forth or moving within or away from New York City; a migrant floating about the country as the crops and seasons dictate. There are Spanish Americans who are more or less settled in one place, one home; but most of them are much more mobile than the general American population, which is itself in considerable flux.

For this man in triple suspension, the church must serve as interpreter and as bridge. No other institution has the facilities, the understanding, the personnel, the interest that the church has in giving the Spanish American an "at-homeness" in two cultures at once, in bringing harmony to the conflicting generations, and in helping the newcomer to adjust to his new environment. This is a difficult task, for Spanish Americans are in various stages of transition. What will work with one group or one individual will not necessarily work with another. The church and the ministry must be prepared to adapt themselves to the given situation. In one church, for example, the ministers may need to be primarily concerned about the stabilizing of family life. It could be that in such a situation the older generation is too protective of the girls of the Spanish American community, cutting them off from a normal and needed relationship with young men. The Reverend William Wendt of St. Christopher's Chapel, Trinity Parish, New York City, suggests that in such a situation, "The churches can and should provide an adequate social program where the boys and girls can meet in a healthy relationship." Such programs would not only solve serious social problems for young women but could also keep young Spanish American men from becoming users of narcotics and members of gangs.

In other situations the stage of transition may require bilingual worship services, Bible classes, Sunday school classes, laboratories in skills and crafts. A middle-aged Spanish American said to his pastor, "If you begin to preach in English, I shall not want to come to church. You will not be reaching me." The pastor replied, "Ah, *mi hermano* (my brother), if I do not preach in English, I shall not be reaching your son." Son and father must be reached, and the church must provide the gospel in the language in which it can be understood.

Except for those Anglo-American churches that have only a few Spanish American communicants—and these English-speaking—all churches that seek to minister to a Spanish American community should provide a bilingual ministry. This is true for the Anglo-American church that seeks to minister to a nearby Spanish American community, and it is also true for those churches that are exclusively Spanish-speaking. Even though the local church is Spanish-speaking, the world around it is not. The minister and his lay staff must frequently serve as the liaison between the two worlds. The purpose is not to translate one language into another but to interpret both worlds, both cultures, to the man in the middle, so that he may maintain his balance between the two. The purpose is not to force an Anglo-American culture upon Spanish Americans as rapidly as possible but to make it possible for them to preserve and blend in themselves the best of both cultures.

Nevertheless, we must not underestimate the need for Spanish-speaking churches. There are numerous communities and small cities in the United States where more than 50 per cent of the people prefer Spanish to English and where a smaller percentage speak little or no English. Obviously, it is futile for the Anglo-American churches to insist that those people attend English-language services. Alfonso Rodriguez has said: "The church is not fulfilling its function to serve the community if it merely invites Spanish-speaking people to integrate. They need still to be served and ministered unto in their own language as a part of the total ministry and the total congregation of the church." The question is not what language the people speak but whether the gospel is being made intelligible to them, whether they are receiving a gracious, but not patronizing, welcome into the Christian fellowship, and whether that fellowship, to the best of its ability, is ministering to their total need.

It may be true that the existence of the ethnic church perpetuates the isolation of Spanish Americans from the Anglo-American community and may symbolize the estrangement of the two ethnic groups. This, however, is a risk that must be run in conveying the gospel to a people who cannot receive it in English. Moreover, this is a problem that time will resolve as, under pressure from the acculturating young people, the Spanish-language church becomes a bilingual church and the bilingual church becomes an English-language church. In the end, the church that began with a strict ethnic identity will probably be absorbed by the larger church now dominated by Anglo-Americans. This has been the experience with Swedish American, German American, Norwegian American churches. For good or ill, and perhaps over a longer period of time, this will probably be the history of Spanish American churches. Meanwhile, the gospel must be preached and taught, and Spanish is a language beautiful, precise, and efficient for proclamation.

Moreover, despite the danger of creating an ethnic church and of weakening denominational loyalties, Spanish-speaking churches must not be condemned or hindered if they establish associations with one another across denominational lines. These associations need not be clannish and need not threaten the ties binding those churches to their parent bodies. They give the Spanish-speaking churches a sense of oneness and strength in an inhospitable religious setting. Such organizations as the Asociación Bautista Lagunera to which Spanish-speaking Baptist churches in Chicago belong and the interdenominational Asociación de Iglesias Evangélicas de Chicago serve a need that is not being met in any other way. So long as that need exists—a need for community, which the Anglo-American churches are either unable or unwilling to meet—associations of Spanish-speaking churches are essential and should be neither criticized nor restricted by denominational authorities.

The tensions that come from living constantly between several worlds, times, and places in a land that is in many ways hostile to him, is wearying and nerve wearing. Under such stresses, the Spanish American is tempted to turn in upon himself and his kind, to find his security in his own group, and his reassurance in his own language. This is not entirely bad, yet, taken to extremes, it merely compounds his problem. The role of the church is to lead this person out of the emotional, as well as the physical, ghetto, to help him find his way into mainstream American life without stripping from him all the vestiges of a culture that he cherishes. As Miss Ellorin wrote about The Riverside Church (see page 111), the church can and should become "a magnificent opportunity for those people who want to become integrated into the community in which they reside and adapt themselves to the plane of the society in which they live." Few churches, to be sure, have at their doorsteps so many Spanish American people and are so well equipped to serve them as is The Riverside Church. But no church that borders on, or is immersed in, a Spanish American community is so small that it cannot perform for Spanish Americans suspended between cultures, generations, and localities an interpreter's duty to bring understanding and communication where there is fear, suspicion, and estrangement. Specifically, the local church can assist Spanish Americans in legal matters, before the courts, in their housing and employment problems, in mediating community quarrels and juvenile gang fights, in learning English, in all their adjustments to a new life.

. . . *"Barrio" to Slum*

Earlier we noted the tight community life, the village or *barrio* setting out of which most Spanish Americans moved into the towns and cities of the United States. The Spanish American has not been able to take with him into his new setting the organization, the security, the intimacy of the *barrio*. His new environment has none of the structure, the comforts, or the disciplines of his village. The block on which he lives, disorganized and impersonal, affords him no protection, no forum for self-expression, no organization for concerted community action. Here the church can serve as the social center that gives structure to the disorganized lives of Spanish American newcomers, that provides in its group meetings a forum in which they can express themselves, that includes them in an established community, and that promotes the development of the Spanish American leadership so greatly needed.

In such a setting the church—stable, fixed, enduring—should become the wholesome social cosmos for otherwise detached, fragmented, and purposeless Spanish American life. Unless the church seizes this opportunity, less highly motivated forces—gangs, unscrupulous politicians, divisive community organizations—will step into the vacuum and will for their own ends, rather than for the ends of the Spanish Americans, organize and administer disjoined Spanish American sectors of American cities. This could be tragic not only for Spanish Americans but also for the churches and for the commonwealth. One of the big sociological questions of our day is this: Who will bring order and unity to the jungles of our inner cities? Increasingly, Spanish Americans and the churches will play principal roles in this drama. But if the churches do no more in the ghettos of the great metropolitan centers and in the slum sections of the smaller cities than they are now doing; if they continue to retreat to the safe suburbs, building lush new churches there but leaving no witness, no service, no community behind them; if they despair of the people who have already in such large numbers despaired of themselves—if this continues, it is not difficult to predict the outcome of the struggle for the depressed areas of metropolitan America. And what is involved is not just geographic areas but people, every one of whom is a child of God and worthy of all that Christ's church can do for him.

.   .   .   *Additional Items*

To these suggestions we must add a few specific proposals for the Protestant ministry to Spanish Americans, suggesting actions that must have priority on the churches' schedule. First, it is plain that the greatest need in the Protestant-Spanish American relationship is for knowledge and understanding on the part of both Spanish and Anglo-Americans. *The Texas Presbyterian* for December, 1959, made the correct analysis: "Information is scarce, communication is poor, statistics are incomplete, and, as a result, interest has been negligible." What this church organ said about its own denomination's relationship to Spanish Americans can with equal pertinence be applied to most Protestant denominations, and to the Roman Catholic Church as well. And to the lack of information, communication, and statistics we must add the lack of personal contact between Anglo-Americans and Spanish Americans.

In its January, 1960, issue *The Texas Presbyterian* showed

what can happen as the result of the alienation of Spanish and Anglo-Americans from each other—even when both groups are Christian:

Even though the Latin American churches do share some of the same problems of Anglo churches of comparable size, the "different" label has stuck. It's no wonder that it has—not because the churches are different but because the people (the Anglos) just don't know too much about them. . . . Some of the Latin-Anglo gulf is because of language and cultural differences. But a good part of the misunderstanding can be blamed on the Anglos who still look upon the Latin church as only a mission—another item in the benevolence budget. And, as a by-product of this, the Anglos figuratively pat the churches (Spanish American) on the head, give them a Christmas basket, and tell them just what they should do to solve their problem.

This void must be bridged, and nothing short of a massive educational program by all the churches—as much in concert as possible—will narrow the gap of ignorance and misunderstanding dividing Spanish American and Anglo-American Christians. For some churches in areas where there are no Spanish-speaking people, this education will necessarily be academic; it is nevertheless necessary. It is especially important that the introduction of Anglo-Americans and Spanish Americans to each other in areas where there are communities of Spanish Americans be something more than academic. Christians from both sides of the ethnic line must meet one another in shared worship, common meals, mutual Christian endeavors, united community campaigns, and in all such encounters that break down the barriers of ignorance and suspicion and that cultivate the ties of Christian fellowship.

Second, the denominations will not be taking their responsibility for Spanish Americans seriously until the resources of those denominations are more generously channeled toward this work. Other needs that we have noted—

adequate buildings, a trained ministry, Spanish-language literature, etc.—require a much larger share of the mission budgets than has thus far been given to them. These needs on the one side and the challenging opportunities on the other are a strong plea for the concentration of funds in the development of Spanish American churches. Two notes of caution: As much as possible, the funds made available for Spanish American churches should be matched by the funds and services of Spanish Americans, minimizing the paternalistic approach and developing self-supporting Spanish American churches as rapidly as possible. Also, the immensity and the complexity of the need and opportunity suggest the need for a master, interdenominational strategy. Working singly and without knowledge of, or concern about, the activities of other churches, denominations will tend to saturate one area and neglect another. The rise of independent churches cannot be regulated, and there should be no attempt to do so, but the major denominations—particularly those that are members of the National Council of Churches—should pool their planning and coordinate the dispersal of their funds.

Third, Anglo-American Protestants should invest not only their money but also their manpower in Spanish American churches, a kind of integration in reverse. It is not every Anglo-American, of course, who has the linguistic ability to make the necessary adjustment to a Spanish-speaking religious community and at the same time make a worthy contribution to the life of that community. Mr. and Mrs. Roger D. Conklin of Downers Grove, Illinois—a young Spanish-speaking Anglo-American couple—have for several years been members of the Central Spanish Church of Chicago. They consider this membership a blessing to them, rather than a sacrificial venture. In turn, they provide talent that is greatly needed and give this church a valuable tie with the Anglo-American world.

Living in the suburbs that fringe our great metropolitan centers are thousands of young men and women whose Christian devotion is not satisfied by services that can be rendered in their neighborhoods, who have talents needed by churches in the city, and who could have an exciting, deeply rewarding experience by belonging to and working in the inner city church. If such young couples know a little Spanish or are willing to learn, a struggling Spanish American church will give them an opportunity for service and, as the Conklins have so well put it, they will get more out of that kind of church membership than they can possibly put into it.

This opportunity is not restricted to the metropolitan centers but is available in the Southwest in hundreds of cities and towns. Anglo-American young people who volunteer for this kind of lay ministry should not go to the Spanish American church as though they were on a mission, nor should they go believing that they have everything to contribute and nothing to gain. If the spirit moves them in this direction, they should cast in their whole lot with the Spanish American church, ready to give and to receive, to minister and to be ministered unto. If they go in this spirit, they can be assured of a whole-hearted welcome and an unparalleled opportunity to serve Christ where the need is real and great.

Fourth, one of the weakest links in the Protestant ministry to Spanish Americans is the scarcity of Spanish American ministers and the even more critical lack of educated ministers. The dearth of qualified ministers that the Presbyterian Church, U.S., confessed may describe an extreme situation but it is not unique. The shortage of qualified ministers for Spanish American churches is serious and is not getting better. Meanwhile, the Spanish American population in the United States increases, the Spanish American community grows more hospitable to the Protestant gospel; and the de-

mand for Spanish American ministers outruns the supply.
The problem is compounded by the fact that the educational
level of many Spanish American laymen is rising, and they
find it increasingly difficult to grant professional status to
ministers among them who have not had formal theological
training.

We are facing here a deficiency that cannot be corrected
immediately. The recruitment of candidates for the ministry
must begin at the high school level through denominational
programs shaped specifically to attract young Spanish-speaking Americans to the Protestant ministry. Although the
motivation toward the Christian ministry should not be
financial, it can be predicted that the recruitment of young
men for the Spanish American ministry will become increasingly difficult unless the churches establish minimum salary
plans that give young Spanish American ministers a chance
to live with at least a minimum of comfort and to pursue
their careers in dignity.

Fifth, the success of the Protestant mission to Spanish
Americans depends upon a more evangelistic ministry by
Spanish Americans themselves. The wife of one Spanish
American minister, commenting on the slow progress of
their church, said, "Our people do not seem to know how
to get out and visit, to invite a neighbor to church, to talk to
others about church. One answer is that they are afraid that
their neighbor or friend is Catholic." The minister said, "We
must not blame the evangelistic failure all on the culture or
Catholicism of Latin Americans. We must blame ourselves
for a lack of zeal and planning." Actually this is no reflection
on the spirit within most Spanish American churches—
which usually runs high—but reflects a reticence on the congregation's part to take the Christian joys it experiences beyond its own bounds.

In the last analysis, the evangelizing of Spanish Americans
is as much the duty and the privilege of Spanish Americans

as it is of Anglo-Americans. Anglo-Americans must cross the ethnic barrier and sometimes the racial and linguistic barriers in evangelizing Spanish Americans. Spanish American Christians, on the other hand, have none of these problems and can achieve among their own people a ready hearing that Anglo-Americans achieve only with considerable difficulty. Moreover, the Spanish American who approaches a member of his own community with the gospel of Jesus Christ is in himself the proof that one can become a Protestant without becoming an Anglo-American and without surrendering cherished aspects of the Spanish American culture. This does not relieve Anglo-Americans of their Christian duty to Spanish Americans, nor does it cut them off from enriching fellowship with Spanish American Christians. It merely distributes the responsibility as it must be distributed if the opportunity that is now opening to Protestants is to be successfully grasped.

· · ·   *The Visiting Student*

So far as their religious orientation is concerned, three kinds of students come from the southern nations to secure an education in the United States. Some are devout Roman Catholics. They will not be converted to Protestantism in significant numbers, but the attitudes that they develop toward Protestantism in this country and that they later disseminate in their own lands—if those attitudes are favorable—can help liberalize governmental and community attitudes toward Protestant missions and toward the Protestant nationals. It is imperative that these students not return to their homelands. convinced that Protestantism is a culture religion, that its people are racial bigots, that Protestantism is an adjunct of imperialism and exploitation, and that it is superficial to the lives of those people who give it their verbal allegiance.

A second group of students from Central and South American countries come to the schools of this country wearing the name of the Roman Catholic Church but are actually secularists who, in deference to relatives or with a kind of cultural reflex action, identify themselves as Roman Catholics. These students resist the appeal of any religion that demands a primary and exclusive allegiance. Again, their personal need for the Christian faith is their chief claim upon the Protestant churches and particularly upon the campus witnesses provided by those churches. Perhaps the churches should concentrate upon these young people and their need and let the international effect of that ministry take care of itself. The fact remains that these young people and their views of Protestantism—whether they become Protestants or not—will have a determinative impact upon the spread of the Protestant witness in lands that are dominated by the Roman Catholic Church but in which the majority of the people are only nominally Roman Catholic. Catholicism has had its chance with the young people and has failed. What Protestantism will do with its opportunity to win an intelligent but religiously cynical or indifferent youth who come north for their education is even now in process of being determined by the kind of Protestant ministry offered to these young people.

The third group of students coming from the southern nations to the universities and colleges of the United States is composed of Protestant youth who, in the main, enroll in church related colleges. The colleges these students attend are selected not only because they are good educational institutions but also because they are assumed to be religious institutions. Four years in a United States college can be a disillusioning experience for Protestant young people from devoutly Christian homes in Central and South America. The college experience is often disillusioning for young people—whatever the native country or the home from which they come. The college age is usually one in which young people begin to develop skepticism about religion and rebellion against parental authority.

Many of the Central and South American students encounter an additional temptation in colleges and universities in the United States. They come not only from homes that still practice strict family and social codes in a tradition inherited from Spain, but they also come, in many cases, from Protestant homes that observe a strict Christian discipline. The free and sophisticated air on the campuses of the United States—even in church related and church controlled schools—can be a shock to young people raised in a much more cloistered environment than the one they meet in this country. It is not the duty of the churches and campus ministries to keep these young people cloistered, to protect them from blasts of Anglo-American cynicism and sophistication, or to deprive them of those rigorous mental exercises that are a part of their education. But it is the duty of the churches and the campus ministries to cultivate in these young men and women a Christian faith and a personal morality that will survive their introduction to the superficial and ephemeral qualities of North American life. It is the duty of the churches to see to it that young people who are simultaneously experiencing in themselves the collision of Spanish and Anglo-American cultures and the clash of a casual morality against the Christian disciplines in which they have been raised are guided into the deeper experiences of the Christian faith. Without pampering these students or protecting them from experiences essential to their education, the churches, campus ministries, faculties, and administrative officers of church schools can deepen, rather than destroy, the faith of these visiting Protestant students. If they perform this duty, the students will on their return to their homelands immensely strengthen the Protestant witness.

The response of the churches to Central and South Ameri-

can students attending colleges and universities in the United
States has therefore a dual motivation. First is the double
ministry of witness and service to young men and women
far from home and immersed in a strange culture. Their
need for the gospel, for acceptance, for counseling, and, in
some instances, for financial support is both a challenge to,
and an opportunity for, the Protestant churches to perform
a ministry that seeks only the good of those to whom the
ministry is offered. Second, such a ministry produces far
reaching advantages for the Protestant mission in Latin
America, sending back to their native countries young men
and women who are destined for influential roles in their
nation's life, and who return, in some cases, with their Protestant view of the Christian life strengthened, and, in other
cases, with their former indifference or antagonism to Protestantism wholesomely modified. This must always be the
secondary rather than the primary motivation of Protestants
in their ministry to Latin American students in colleges and
universities in the United States. Nevertheless, it will be a
tragedy for Protestantism if the churches forfeit this opportunity to send to Central and South American nations mes-
sengers of good will toward the Protestant mission in this
part of the Western Hemisphere.

.   .   .   *In a Word*

We have confessed that thus far the ministry to
Spanish Americans has been lamentably inadequate and that
this shameful neglect has been due primarily to ignorance and
misunderstanding and a consequent dearth of vision and concern on the part of Anglo-Americans. We have noted four
programs that work: active evangelism; social welfare services
in the broadest concept of the term; community activities—
such as clubs, sports, recreation centers—that take advantage
of the yearning of young Spanish Americans to be identified
with the mainstream of American history; and the inesti-

mably valuable witness of Anglo-American Christian families that demonstrate in their daily contact with Spanish Americans the inclusive love of Jesus Christ. Moreover, we have seen that the Protestant ministry to Spanish Americans must be shaped to their multiple needs: their longing for acceptance, their respect for the person, their desire to carry with them into Protestantism many of the cherished values and customs of a Spanish American culture, their need for leadership and organization, their deep flowing religiosity, their hunger for a faith that satisfies that religiosity, and their basic deficiencies in employment, housing, health, and education.

In part, we have suggested that a Protestant ministry addressed to those needs must be a mutual enterprise in which Spanish and Anglo-Americans share the duties and privileges of this ministry, working together to foster independent, self-supporting, Spanish-speaking, and bilingual churches on the one hand, and, on the other hand, keeping Anglo-American churches open and hospitable to Spanish Americans who desire to belong to such churches. This mutual enterprise must concentrate on a massive educational program to remove the barriers of ignorance and prejudice in both groups and to create of the two groups a true Christian community. The immensity and the delicacy of the task require an ecumenical approach and supervision. Where denominations can best pursue their own programs of witness and service, there should be a coordination of these programs to eliminate waste, competition, and, in the minds of the Spanish Americans, confusion.

We have noted in a general way that the funds apportioned by the denominations for one of the greatest needs and the greatest opportunity on the home mission scene are paltry, and that such funds—especially for the subsidizing of the salaries of Spanish American ministers; the renovating and building of adequate churches, missions, set-

tlement houses, schools, clinics; the production of a complete Spanish-language religious literature (not merely trans-
lations from English but original works designed particularly
for the Spanish American community)—must be many times
multiplied if the need is to be met and the opportunity accepted. In a word, Spanish Americans present Protestantism
with a conjunction of need and opportunity—a challenge to
witness, service, and unity—unparalleled on this continent
and in this generation.

PART THREE

Receiving from Spanish Americans

◄§ 8 WHAT SPANISH AMERICANS CAN CONTRIBUTE

. . . *Revitalizing American Protestantism*

It is a well known fact of Christian history that the church not only continues through its natural heirs but also is revived and reformed by its adopted children. That is, the church has its continuity in the descendants of its Christian families in a kind of Lois to Eunice to Timothy progression. And, not always but frequently, it has its revitalization through the conversion and the adoption of the children of the non-Christian neighbors. For example, in the first century of this era a Jewish Christianity, in danger of becoming an obscure Jewish sect, received a powerful forward thrust when Paul and his companions took the gospel to the Greeks and the Romans, and when Peter, after seeing a vision, finally approved the mission to the gentiles. Or, much later, when Rome was falling and the church was threatening to fall with it, barbarians converted to Jesus Christ supplied a revitalization of the church and guaranteed its survival. Today a decadent Christianity looks to the young churches of Asia and Africa for the insight, the vision, and the devotion that can renew the church.

This has been the story: The church has progressed, has periodically risen to new life, not by a purist exclusion of gentiles—non-Christians—but by welcoming converted non-

Christians into the church, receiving in them not only a new
stock but also, and equally important, a new understanding
of the meaning of the gospel, a new zeal and a new piety.
It is the gentile who, won to Christ and embraced by his
body, the church, restores to Christianity its primitive vitality. So the church evangelizes beyond the families of the
church, or it perishes. It sends missionaries and makes
disciples of all nations, or it withers, retaining its form but
losing its spirit. It wins the stranger, the alien, the newcomer, or it becomes so caked by its institutionalizing, so
hardened in its growing old that it is unequal to the challenge of the world. Nowhere is it more clearly demonstrated
than in the history of the church that it is in giving that
we receive and, dying unto ourselves, live. If the blood of the
martyrs is the seed of the church, then mission in witness
and service is the nourishment of the church. Our Lord said,
"My food is to do the will of him who sent me." He was
saying that the thing that restored him and built him up was
obedience to the Father's will. If that was true for him, it is
none the less true for the church, which is his body. The
food of the church—that which restores and renews it—is
doing the will of the Father. And it is the Father's will that
we bring disciples of all nations to his Son.

We should know by now—certainly we have been repeat-
edly told—that Protestantism suffers today from poor health.
Despite all the outward evidences—the building of new
churches in unparalleled numbers at unprecedented costs and
the swelling membership rolls—Protestantism in the United
States looks inward and is unhappy about what it sees. It
sees in itself a religion that more and more takes on the
coloration of society and that is increasingly identified with
upper- and middle-class America. These are signs of decay.
How can this decay be arrested? How can it be replaced by
a new spiritual growth? There are several possible answers to
this question, several needed remedies. But few of these

remedies lie so close at hand, are so available and potentially so fruitful as two: the resolving of the racial division of the church and a Protestant embrace of Spanish Americans. The redemption of American Protestantism—the flush of success on its outward features and decay in its soul—waits upon the closing of the gap, the healing of the wound between white Christians and Negro Christians, and it waits upon the meeting of Spanish Americans and Anglo-Americans in the same Protestant church.

The white Protestant churches in the United States need a new stock to free them from their middle-class prison. They need the new insights of such a stock to free them from the stifling genteel mentality and the prim and proper morality of an affluent, status-seeking culture. It could well be that in the end Spanish Americans—who must be our sole interest here—will do more for Protestantism than Protestantism does for Spanish Americans. Spanish Americans offer Protestant churches an opportunity to serve and be served and in the process to be redeemed and revived. We need to ask therefore in what way other than numerically Spanish American Christians can contribute to the revival of American Protestantism. Although the ministry of Protestant churches to Spanish Americans should not be motivated by anticipated returns, we have the right and the need to ask in what ways Spanish Americans who are won to the Christian life in Protestant churches can correct the current deficiencies of Anglo-Protestantism.

. . . *Correlative Benefits*

It should be mentioned in passing that there are many indirect contributions that Spanish Americans make to Protestantism that cannot be dealt with at length here. Most studies of the history of the United States have grossly underestimated and, in some cases, ignorantly misrepresented the contributions that Spanish Americans have made to the composite American identity. Habitually, we have traced the development of this country—its ideologies, customs, religion, economy, and industry—from seventeenth century beginnings on the East Coast westward to the Pacific Coast. Unquestionably, this has been the dominant stream of American culture. In large part, we have ignored the contribution that the American Negro made to this westward-sweeping American history. Even more thoroughly we have disregarded the impact that a Spanish Indian culture made upon a region of the United States much vaster than the original thirteen colonies. Let us remember that before Jamestown and Plymouth Rock there were Spanish settlements in what are now New Mexico and California. The influence of these settlements on the Southwest as they multiplied, spread, and through intermarriage and absorption adopted portions of the indigenous Indian civilization was deep and persistent. Here was a culture that impressed its language on a vast territory that later became part of the United States and that gave Spanish names to hundreds of villages, towns, and cities in that wide area. Here was a culture that set fashions in dress, art, music, and architecture; that created a distinct pattern of village planning and community life; that introduced to that area the horse, the gun, the church, and various crops. The Spanish Indian culture, then, has contributed significantly to the composite American identity and has indirectly contributed to the lives of Protestants, if not to their religion. (Readers who want to pursue this thought are referred to the bibliography.)

A second fact too important to ignore is that Spanish Americans of the United States can be of inestimable value to their country in its political approach to the countries of the south and to their churches in their South American mission. This is not due to the fact that Spanish Americans are Spanish-speaking. Some of them do not speak Spanish— at least, not a correct, fluent Spanish—and some Anglo-

Americans do speak good Spanish. The advantage that Spanish Americans have in the bridge-building process—whether political or missionary—is that they are Spanish Americans. They do not have to overcome the barriers of distrust and suspicion that economic imperialism and exploitation have erected between the South and Central American and the Anglo-American.

The political situation in the Caribbean, for example, is a serious one, fraught with all kinds of problems for the United States and every kind of mischief for Central and South America. Serious as the situation is, it would be critical and perhaps irreparable were it not for the fact that Communist-controlled Cuba is matched in the Caribbean by a democratic Puerto Rico, which voluntarily chooses a commonwealth relationship with the United States. There are two giants in the Caribbean: Fidel Castro and Luis Muñoz Marín: the first, the avowed Marxist who is a prisoner of the Communist bloc; and the second, the democrat who voluntarily cooperates with but is not controlled by the United States. These political giants and their programs for the economic rescue of their people are closely watched throughout Central and South America.

Puerto Rico demonstrates to the southern nations that it is possible to have a relationship with the United States that is not exploitative and that leaves the people free to determine their own destiny even while they receive assistance from the United States for their economic recovery. Puerto Ricans, in this country as well as in their native island, are the best possible bridge between the United States and the southern nations, and the treatment that the island receives from the United States Government and that its people receive when they exercise a citizen's privilege of moving to this country will determine whether that bridge stands or falls. If the United States has a sincere, honest word of mutual cooperation and mutual helpfulness to speak to its southern neighbors, it should as much as possible use Spanish Americans to speak that word.

Similarly, our several denominations that have missionary work in Central and South America should recruit and train an increasing number of Spanish American Protestants for the vast missionary frontier that in the past half-century has opened in that area to the Protestant witness. To a people who have long believed that religion and culture are identical —even when they maintain no ties at all with the church— it is advantageous to send the gospel through Spanish American Protestants who are living and convincing evidence that Protestantism and Anglo-American culture are not identical. The Spanish American minister is much more successful than the Anglo-American in convincing Spanish-speaking people that one need not become a renegade or a traitor to *la raza* (the race) when he leaves behind his vague, non-institutional Roman Catholicism and becomes a Protestant.

It is the Spanish American Protestant also who can best shatter the stereotype that represents Protestantism as cold, colorless, and negatively moralistic. This stereotype exists in the minds of many Central and South American churches primarily because Protestant sects and sometimes the mainline Protestant churches have planted and fostered this false symbol of Protestantism. The speed with which the Protestant witness is accepted in Central and South America depends in part upon the elimination of the stereotype. Protestant Spanish Americans who are devout yet not dour, personally disciplined yet happy in their faith, are Protestantism's best witness to the fact that the joyful life and Christian piety, in the best sense of the word, are not mutually exclusive.

The penetration of the culture barrier between Protestantism and the peoples of southern nations will also be facilitated by a wise and concerned Protestant ministry to Central and South American students attending colleges in the United States every year. Since many of these young men and women will become in a few years the leaders and molders of public opinion in their own countries, the impression of Protestantism that they carry home with them will help determine the reception that the Protestant churches receive in their homelands. They will take with them not so much what they hear about Protestantism as what they see in Protestant lives.

These collateral benefits are too important to be omitted from our reference to Spanish American contributions. They help us see that the flow of values is not from Anglo-Americans to Spanish Americans only, but is two-directional. The Spanish-Anglo-American encounter within the United States can be mutually helpful or mutually harmful. It will be mutually harmful if Anglo-Americans assume that in the encounter they have everything to give and nothing to receive, everything to teach and nothing to learn.

So, preparatory to a look at the deeper values Spanish Americans can bring to Protestantism, we have noted the cultural contributions Spanish Americans have made and are making to the composite American identity. We have mentioned the services that Spanish Americans can render in building the international bridges between the United States and Central and South American countries. Similarly, we stressed the importance of using Spanish American Protestants in the churches' mission to Central and South American countries. Finally, we have noted the importance of the Protestant ministry to students who come to the colleges and universities in the United States from Central and South American countries, stressing the value of this ministry to the students themselves and the importance of the attitudes of these students to the Protestant mission in Latin America. It is important that we recognize the fact that in these areas Spanish Americans have an enormous contribution to make to the culture of this nation, to its relationship to all of

Latin America, and to the Protestant mission in Central and South America. We turn now to consider those spiritual contributions that strong Spanish American customs and insights can make toward the revitalization of Anglo-American Protestantism.

. . .   *What Anglo-American*
                               Protestantism Needs

A brief reminder of the current deficiencies of Anglo-American Protestantism will help us see more clearly what Spanish American Protestants and certain Spanish customs can contribute to the revival of that Protestantism. In the first place, Anglo-American Protestantism is fantastically affluent. Despite the fact that there are some local churches that struggle along on meager and inadequate budgets and despite the fact that some churches live beyond their income in a keeping-up-with-the-Joneses race, most Protestant churches in the United States are wealthy in comparison with their past and in contrast with Christian churches in other lands. They are tempted by and often succumb to all of the dangers of wealth: smugness, materialistic evaluations, self-centeredness, detachment from and indifference to the needs of the poor.

Second, American Protestantism is numerically prosperous. Since World War II, the membership of most Protestant denominations has grown phenomenally. This growth, however, is deceiving. The depth and genuineness of it are difficult to test. But we know that it has occurred in an age that equates church membership with social acceptability and in which "the American way of life" requires at least a nominal church affiliation. This popularization of religion has required and has helped promote a softening of Christianity's moral imperatives and a modifying of its theological uniqueness and radicalness. The result—variously labelled and defined—is known popularly as a vague, puerile, superficial religion-in-general. What an editor of *The Christian Century* saw approaching a quarter of a century ago and called "amorphous religiosity" has now arrived. An artificial, anti-Christian blending of Christ and culture—a periodic heresy in the church's history—has robbed the church and the gospel of their vitality and has robbed Christian life of its zeal and devotion.

Third, Anglo-American Protestantism has captured and has been captured by the middle and upper-middle classes in American society. There are exceptions, to be sure. There are churches that minister primarily to people of low income and education, and in most affluent churches there will be a few needy people. But in the main, the Protestant churches in the United States occupy and serve the middle strata of American society. They are socially as well as racially homogeneous. Such churches become ingrown and soon confuse the people's economic, social, and political interest with the gospel. They tend to acquire the coloration and some of the customs of a social club and to lose their distinctiveness from the secular world. In such a setting the Jesus Christ who is Lord of all life is tamed and made the defender of the status quo.

Fourth, Anglo-American Protestantism is fleeing from the inner cities of our great metropolitan complexes to the secure and comfortable suburbs. No doubt the suburbs need the church and the gospel just as much in their own ways as the central cities do in theirs. But in their haste to follow their members—the middle and upper-middle people—to the suburbs, the fleeing churches leave behind little Christian witness or service for the masses of people who flood the inner city. Two obvious questions arise: Who will proclaim the gospel in the slums of our cities, the ghettos, the deteriorating fringe areas, the concrete jungles that rise in redeveloping areas and in all the places "where cross the crowded ways of life"? And, second, who will rescue the Protestant churches

—to use Gibson Winter's phrase—from their suburban captivity? [1]

Fifth, Protestant life, rebelling against puritanism and legalism, has reduced Christian faith and morality to a choice between sentimentalism on the one side and to existential libertinism on the other. Contemporary Protestantism appears to offer men only two ethical options: an emotion-saturated optimism that ignores the peril and tragedy of man's life by bathing him in a faith that is egocentric, self-hypnotizing, and superficial; or a blasé code of morality that permits the Christian to live just as other men do and cast his undisciplined life upon the mercy of an indulgent God. Needed is a code of morality that accepts the fact that nothing we do can win the freely given favor of a loving God but accepts also the fact that God demands of those who receive his grace rigorously disciplined lives that in obedience do his will and in gratitude keep his commandments. Needed are men and women whose freely redeemed lives are lived in glad obedience. That kind of life is rare in contemporary Protestantism.

Sixth, many Protestants have lost their confidence in Jesus Christ as the unique, universal, and final Savior and Lord of men. Looking around, they do not see "Jesus only" but many holy men and many sacred teachings, and they conclude that the way to true and relevant religion is through a multiple allegiance to several of these holy men—including Jesus Christ—and through a compilation of the best insights of several scriptures. With a basket on their arms they roam the field of world religions and the history of American folklore, picking up a bright object here, an interesting item there, filling the basket. The accumulation they shake vigorously, thoroughly mixing the items, and call the result their religion. Whatever this may be, it is not Christianity.

---

[1] Winter, Gibson. *The Suburban Captivity of the Churches.* Garden City, N.Y.: Doubleday & Co., Inc., 1961.

The Christian faith demands an undivided acceptance of, and obedience to, Jesus Christ as Lord and Savior. It is imperial in its claims, arbitrary in its proclamations, and exclusive of all rivals who in any way modify the uniqueness, the universality, and the finality of Jesus Christ. The acknowledgment and acceptance of such a Christ, such a faith, is essential to the revival of Protestantism.

In these six ways, and to a lesser extent in others, the reforming branch of Christianity itself needs reformation. Our question now is: In what ways and to what extent can Spanish American Protestants contribute to the needed revival of Anglo-American Protestantism? Obviously, we must not lay the responsibility for this revitalization of decadent churches upon Spanish Americans and expect them to perform some miracle for Anglo-Protestant benefit. Obviously also, we cannot predict with certainty what will happen as more and more Spanish Americans enter the Protestant stream. Will they make a corrective impact upon the church or be absorbed and dissipated by it? What we can do is to indicate some Spanish American characteristics that would, if adopted, aid the reformation of Protestantism and point to certain attributes of Spanish American communities that could be redemptive if adopted by Anglo-American Protestants.

. . .   *Varieties of Gifts*

We have noted earlier that the Spanish American moves into the mainstream of American culture bearing within himself a religious sense of life. It is easy to make more of this than we should, to exaggerate the religiosity that is characteristic of most Spanish Americans. Yet it remains true that Spanish Americans, whether formally religious or not, whether prochurch or antichurch, view and affirm life "in terms of its spiritual values and move closer to an acceptance of life's religious sense. Their voice is that of the Hispanic-

American race, whose intellectual tradition is a variation on
the theme of spiritualism." [2] Ramos calls our attention to a
Spenglerian saying: "Only Faustian Man thinks, feels, and
lives in its (technology's) forms. For him that technology is
a *spiritual* necessity." [3] We can go further with the generalization that for the Anglo-American the capitalistic economy and the scientific view of life, in addition to technology,
are spiritual necessities. This is not to say that the Anglo-
American is irreligious; it is to say that his life—his concepts,
his purposes, his enterprises, his values, his behavior—is not
dominated by the religious view. The final arbiter for him is
not religion but something else. Ramos put it rather bluntly:
"Practicality, money, machines, and speed are the things
which provoke the greatest enthusiasm in modern man." [4]
They are not only his greatest enthusiasms but also the cri-
teria of life's values.

Admittedly, this is a grossly oversimplified description, as
is our definition of the Spanish American as a religious man
for whom the religious view of life is a spiritual necessity.
But the exaggeration makes the point that for the Anglo-
American religion is one of several spiritual necessities,
whereas for the Spanish American—even when he repudiates
religion, he does so from a religious base and with religious
fervor—religion is *the* spiritual necessity. Plainly, this is not
necessarily a good thing. That is, religiosity can degenerate
into shallow sentimentality, into superstition, into preoccupa-
tion with the occult. Detached from all institutions, it can
lose sharpness and become a vague suffusion. We are therefore not saying that the Spanish American view of man and
his environment is ideal, flawless, and without dangers. We

---

[2] Ramos, Samuel. *Profile of Man and Culture in Mexico*, p. 89.
Translated by Peter G. Earle. Austin: University of Texas Press, 1962.
(Published in Spanish in 1934)

[3] *Ibid.*, p. 119.

[4] *Ibid.*, p. 98.

are saying rather that Anglo-American and Spanish American Protestants need each other, that their views of man and his needs complement each other. Especially, we are saying at this point that the Spanish American stress upon the function of man's religious spirit can correct the Anglo-American emphasis on technology, science, and enterprise.

Modern Anglo-American man drifts toward a mechanistic view of life: the universe as a great machine and man a cog in that machine. A view of life that has not lost its awareness of the spiritual splendor and terror of the universe, that sees it as God's handiwork and that sees man as consummately a spiritual creature—this view disappears from Anglo-American concepts, even from Protestant minds that should know better. Spanish Americans can help restore that lost concept of man as a multiple but indivisible creature, every part of whom has spiritual meaning and spiritual purpose. Anglo-American Christianity—Protestant and Roman Catholic—has its own brand of religiosity. But that religiosity is a veneer thinly sprayed over the general life. Spanish American religiosity, whatever its deficiencies, is internal to the mood and mind and radiates outward through the general life. Spanish Americans who bring to Protestantism their belief that the religious sense of life is man's chief spiritual necessity can make a significant contribution to the rediscovery of the religious man in a scientific, technological, and economic age. The result will be a restored, enriched, and fulfilled Protestantism. For this understanding of the nature of man, faithfully preserved by the Reformers, has largely disappeared from Anglo-American Protestantism. Protestantism has much to offer Spanish Americans. But its need to be helped is as great as its ability to help. And that need is for a predominant sense of man as a spiritual being.

The second gift that Spanish Americans can contribute to the body of Christ is a Christian affirmation of the dignity of the individual. They can help restore to Protestantism that sense of personal worth and integrity that was once central in non-Roman Catholic thought but that has diminished under the impact of depersonalizing forces in Western civilization. During the past century, the people of the United States have lived under titanic cultural pressures—a rapidly industrialized economy, a swift westward migration, the inheritance of international leadership at a crucial period in human history, recurring war, the East-West tension, pounding mass media. Such forces obscure the individual. He loses his identity, his self-awareness, his sense of a personal worth that is his alone, apart from the meaning of the crowd. He is pulverized and blended into a mass man. The Protestant man has not escaped those depersonalizing pressures any more than has the Roman Catholic or the secularist. Theologically, abstractly, he affirms the worth of the individual, but actually he is captured by a culture that makes robots of men, that favors conformity, and that grows increasingly intolerant of dissident ideas and deviant acts. The lone individual—worthy in himself for his own sake as a child of God and not merely as a tender of machines—is absorbed and dissipated by a monstrous collectiveness.

There are two reasons why Spanish Americans have not suffered as much from these depersonalizing influences as has the general American public. In the first place, the isolation of Spanish Americans within American culture until recent years has protected them from the most severe assaults of a collectivistic culture. The rejections that walled them in have at the same time walled out some of these forces that crush personality. As prisoners of an enclave in American society, Spanish Americans have suffered various and severe deprivations. But the enclave, despite its offenses against the person, has enabled the Spanish Americans to preserve a keener sense of personal integrity and worth than the world outside the enclave permits. The ghetto is always vicious; its crimes against its inhabitants are always greater than any blessings it may bestow upon them. Nevertheless, ghettoization cultivates by its centripetal forces a sharp self-awareness. What will happen to the Spanish American sense of *dignidad* as the people in whom it predominates move into the general society is impossible to predict.

There is another reason why the Spanish American affirmation of personal dignity has durability: It has had a long history; it is plowed into the subconscious. Something of this spirit was depicted three centuries ago by the greatest Spanish writer, Cervantes, in his brain child, Don Quixote. Unfortunately, some people see only the humorous and the ridiculous side of gallant, imaginative, romantic, profoundly religious, wholly individual Don Quixote. But there was a sublime side to this imaginary figure, too. (That, after all, is what man is—a peculiar mixture of the absurd and the sublime.) And one facet of Don Quixote's sublimity—and absurdity—was his self-awareness and his sense of personal worth. This classic literary figure, Don Quixote, rode his nag, Rocinante, not only over Spain on various ventures of knight errantry but also, so to say it, into every land of the Western world where the Spaniard left his language. Don Quixote, the romantic individual, caricatured the Spain of Cervantes' time and endowed New Spain with that same spirit. The personal dignity that this legendary figure sought and championed, sometimes foolishly, his Spanish American descendants still seek and champion, sometimes foolishly, sometimes sublimely.

Perhaps no modern Spaniard has had a keener, at once more painful and more glorious sense of the yearning of every individual to be himself and to persist in being himself than did Miguel de Unamuno. Interestingly enough, he borrowed the germ of this idea of individual integrity from the Dutch Jew, Spinoza; but in Unamuno that germ unfolded in a characteristically and poignantly Spanish fashion. One quotation from Unamuno will convey the fact that we are considering here something deeper than so-called rugged individualism. In the best known of his works, Unamuno writes:

> Everything in me that conspires to break the unity and continuity of my life conspires to destroy me and consequently to destroy itself. Every individual in a people who conspires to break the spiritual unity and continuity of that people tends to destroy it and to destroy himself as a part of that people. What if some other people is better than our own? Very possibly, although perhaps we do not clearly understand what is meant by better or worse. Richer? Granted. More cultured? Granted likewise. Happier? Well, happiness . . . but still, let it pass! . . . Well and good. All this is good—but it is something different. And that is enough. Because for me the becoming other than I am, the breaking of the unity and continuity of my life, is to cease to be he who I am—that is to say, it is simply to cease to be. And that—no! Anything rather than that! [5]

Anyone who cannot understand what Unamuno was driving at cannot understand why Central and South America resist ideas and methods that the United States in its own interests wants to export to these areas and which ideas, if accepted, would break sharply and quickly the continuity of Latin American culture. These words from Unamuno also help us to understand Spanish American "clannishness," wherever it exists, and to appreciate the reluctance of many Spanish Americans to drop the Spanish part of their cultural inheritance as they move into mainstream America. Moreover, through these words we see that Spanish American individualism is not egocentricity, selfishness, or pride but rather a strong sense of the sacredness and the inviolableness of the individual—all individuals.

If Protestantism is looking, as it should be, for deposits of that sense of personal dignity that it once proclaimed and

[5] From *Tragic Sense of Life*, by Miguel de Unamuno, p. 11. Published by Dover Publications, New York 14, N.Y., 1954.

now mutes, it will find no people on the American scene in whom this sense is stronger than it is in Spanish Americans. In this respect, as in others, they have much to teach the Anglo-American Protestant, much to contribute to the whole church. It is expecting a great deal to ask the smaller number of Spanish American Protestants to restore to Anglo-American Protestantism its dwindling sense of the dignity of the individual, but a little leaven can leaven the whole loaf.

A third contribution that Spanish American Protestants can make to the whole church is a practical one that needs only to be mentioned. They can strengthen Protestant witness and service in the inner city. We have already noticed that Spanish Americans who migrate to the big metropolitan areas find themselves, as do most newcomers, temporarily trapped in the poorer, central areas of the cities. These are areas largely deserted by Anglo-American Protestant churches. Spanish American Protestant churches can fill this void, offering a service and a witness that reach beyond the Spanish American community. Out of their own strength, when they have it, or subsidized by home mission boards, Spanish American churches can restore the Protestant witness to the inner city. This will require a bilingual program open to all racial and ethnic groups, a will to minister rather than to be ministered unto, and an inclusive spirit that is willing to sacrifice the ethnic character of the church in a ministry to all people. Spanish American churches in the inner city have, in other words, a parish responsibility. Where they are the only churches in a defined area, all the unchurched people of that area are their Christian responsibility. The acceptance and discharge of this responsibility to the limit of the ability of the Spanish American churches can be a significant contribution to the total Protestant mission.

It has been noted, fourth, that there is a higher degree of Christian piety in Spanish American Protestant communi-

ties than in Anglo-American religious communities, whether
Protestant or Roman Catholic. True, Christian piety is sometimes tempted to concentrate too heavily on the minutiae
of Christian morality. And, likewise, Christian morality
sometimes degenerates into legalism. Yet, apart from these
abuses, Christian piety—the disciplined Christian life—is a
beautiful, powerful, and persuasive evidence that the life that
trusts Christ also seeks to obey him.

To say that Spanish American Protestants live better moral
lives than Anglo-American Protestants is to draw an odious
comparison that cannot be proved one way or the other.
Even so, there is a more open, visible, and unashamed
Christian piety among evangelical Spanish Americans than
there is in the general Protestant population. An exploration
of the reasons for such Christian discipline of the personal
life would take us far afield. In brief, we can say that thus
far the earnestness of Spanish American Protestants has not
been spoiled by the intellectual and social sophistication that
has saturated so much of Anglo-American Protestantism.
Again, converts from one religion to another or from no
religion at all are more likely to be exceptionally faithful in
observing the moral code of their new faith than are other
members of that faith who "inherit" their membership.

Moreover, in Spanish American evangelical piety we see
a genuine Christian expression of Spanish American religiosity. When a vague religious sense of life comes to focus
in a Christian view of life, that view requires that the whole
social and personal life be put under the authority of Jesus
Christ. Finally, we see in the evangelical piety of Spanish
American Protestants a revulsion against the immoralities
tolerated by the Roman Catholic Church wherever it has
been captured in Central and South American countries by
the paganism and politics of those countries. The moral
laxity and indifference of nominal Roman Catholics in Latin
American countries is repudiated by the earnest evangelical

Spanish American. Turning away from that moral laxity and indifference, the Spanish American seeks in embracing Protestantism a piety that not only renounces that kind of Catholicism but that satisfies his spiritual necessity.

Whatever the origin of the disciplined Christian life in the Spanish American community, it has its fundamental precedent and instruction in New Testament teachings. The Christian life can be moral without being moralistic, disciplined without being legalistic, pious without being hypocritical and censorious. The Christian life that knows that it does not deserve, cannot earn, and cannot repay God's gracious act in reconciling all men to him in Jesus Christ and that expresses its gratitude in a conduct willingly obedient to God's will for his children is a rare thing in a cynical and sophisticated culture. Wherever it appears, genuine and humble, it is a challenge to a Protestantism that has lost its sense of values and is too largely content with saying, "Lord, Lord." That kind of life certainly does not appear exclusively in Spanish American Protestant communities, but it does appear there in extraordinary measure. If acculturation does not destroy this Spanish American witness to the good life, this witness can be one of the most significant gifts these Christians can make to the Protestant family.

Finally, Anglo-American Protestants who visit Spanish American Protestant churches are struck by the zeal and enthusiasm that characterize these Christian communities. This, of course, is not universally true; but it is so generally true that genteel, decorous, prim Protestantism would do well to inquire about the origin and the meaning of the prevalent spirit. The contagious vivacity of these communities, like laudable Spanish American piety, may derive from Spanish American religiosity, from the convert's enthusiasm for his new faith, from the primitive vigor of many Spanish American churches, from the fact that Spanish Americans are freer in expressing their emotions than are the more stolid

Anglo-Americans. Such zeal, it should be noted, is neither good nor bad in itself. If undirected, religious zeal can wastefully make itself its own purpose and end. But, on the other hand, Christian zeal and enthusiasm can be the moving of the Holy Spirit through a Christian community, calling it to life, creating its unity, gathering its powers, and sending it into a needful world. Blasé, satiated, stolid Anglo-American Protestantism will not be revived by a mechanically generated enthusiasm; it will be revived if the Holy Spirit is encouraged to move with its quickening powers through Protentantism. Spanish American Protestants who are diligent and zealous in the faith can provide that encouragement.

It has been necessary in this study to make an academic division of the Body of Christ, to write of Spanish American Protestants and Anglo-American Protestants. Were this division not necessary for the purposes of this work, it would be intolerable. We are Christians, some out of one ethnic background and some out of another. We have "gifts that differ according to the grace given to us." These gifts are not bestowed upon us for our exclusive use but are intended for our mutual ministry.

✑§ READING LIST

Leaders of study groups may order the Friendship Press books listed below from denominational literature headquarters. From these same sources they may order the *Adult Guide on "Spanish Americans,"* by Mary Ingram, priced at 75 cents, which contains program plans for using *Death of a Myth* and other Friendship Press publications.

Books of other publishers are listed as additional resources. They are available in bookstores and libraries.

1964 FRIENDSHIP PRESS BOOKS

Martinez, Rafael V. *My House Is Your House.* The cultural background and contributions of Spanish Americans in the United States. Illustrated with photographs.

Taylor, Betty Jo. *Where the Clock Walks.* Stories, quotations, and expository text showing the life and problems of Spanish Americans in the United States. Illustrated with photographs.

ADDITIONAL RESOURCE BOOKS

Abrams, Charles. *Forbidden Neighbors.* New York: Harper & Brothers, 1955.

Alexander, Robert J. *Today's Latin America.* Garden City: Doubleday & Co., Inc. (Anchor Books), 1962.

Ashworth, Mae Hurley, editor. *Who?—Spanish-Speaking Americans in the U.S.A.* New York: Friendship Press, 1953.

Berle, Beatrice Bishop. *80 Puerto Rican Families in New York City.* New York: Columbia University Press, 1958.

Bogardus, Emory S. *The Mexican in the United States.* Los Angeles: University of Southern California Press, 1934.

Burma, John H. *Spanish-Speaking Groups in the United States.* Durham: Duke University Press, 1954.

Gamio, Manuel. *Mexican Immigration to the United States.* Chicago: The University of Chicago Press, 1930.

Graham, Saxon. *American Culture.* New York: Harper & Brothers, 1957.

Griffith, Beatrice. *American Me.* Boston: Houghton Mifflin Co., 1948.

Gruber, Ruth. *Puerto Rico: Island of Promise.* New York: Hill and Wang, 1960.

Gruening, Ernest. *Mexico and Its Heritage.* New York & London: The Century Co., 1928.

Higham, John. *Strangers in the Land: Patterns of American Nativism.* New Brunswick, N.J.: Rutgers University Press, 1955.

Howard, George P. *We Americans: North and South.* New York: Friendship Press, 1951.

Kibbe, Pauline R. *Latin Americans in Texas.* Albuquerque: The University of New Mexico Press, 1946.

Little, Wilson. *Spanish-Speaking Children in Texas.* Austin: The University of Texas Press, 1944.

McHenry, J. Patrick. *A Short History of Mexico.* Garden City: Doubleday & Co., Inc. (Dolphin Books), 1962.

McWilliams, Carey. *North from Mexico: The Spanish-Speaking People of the United States.* Philadelphia and New York: J. B. Lippincott Co., 1949.

Mills, C. Wright and others. *Puerto Rican Journey.* New York: Harper & Brothers, 1950.

Ramos, Samuel. *Profile of Man and Culture in Mexico.* Translated by Peter G. Earle. Austin: The University of Texas Press, 1962. (Published in Spanish in 1934.)

Sánchez, George I. *Forgotten People.* Albuquerque: The University of New Mexico Press, 1940.

Saunders, Lyle. *Cultural Difference and Medical Care: The Case of the Spanish-Speaking People of the Southwest.* New York: Russell Sage Foundation, 1954.

Saunders, Lyle. *The Spanish-Speaking Population of Texas.* Austin: The University of Texas Press, 1949.

Senior, Clarence. *Strangers, Then Neighbors: From Pilgrims to Puerto Ricans.* New York: Freedom Books, 1961.

Shotwell, Louisa R. *The Harvesters: The Story of the Migrant People*. Garden City: Doubleday & Co., Inc., 1961.

Talbert, Robert H. *Spanish-Name People in the Southwest and West*. Fort Worth: Texas Christian University Press, 1955.

Tuck, Ruth D. *Not With the Fist*. New York: Harcourt, Brace and Co., 1946.

Unamuno, Miguel de. *Tragic Sense of Life*. Translated by J. E. Crawford Flitch. New York: Dover Publications, 1954.

Wakefield, Dan. *Island in the City: The World of Spanish Harlem*. Cambridge, Mass.: Houghton Mifflin Co., 1959.

Walter, Paul A. F., Jr. *Race and Culture Relations*. New York: McGraw-Hill Book Co., Inc., 1952.

Whetten, Nathan L. *Rural Mexico*. Chicago: The University of Chicago Press, 1948.

CONFERENCE REPORTS

Summary of Conference on Latin-American Relations in the Southwestern United States. Division of Racial Minorities, The National Council of the Protestant Episcopal Church, 815 Second Avenue, New York 17, N.Y., 1959.

Summary of Conference on Problems of Puerto Ricans in the United States. Home Department, The National Council of the Protestant Episcopal Church, 815 Second Avenue, New York 17, N.Y., 1962.

ABOUT THE FORMAT

TEXT SET IN LINOTYPE ELECTRA, 10 POINT LEADED 2 POINTS.
MANUFACTURED BY THE COLONIAL PRESS INC., CLINTON,
MASSACHUSETTS.
COVERS PRINTED BY AFFILIATED LITHOGRAPHERS, INC., NEW
YORK.
TEXT PAPER, S. D. WARREN'S NUMBER 66 ANTIQUE.
TYPOGRAPHIC DESIGN BY MARGERY W. SMITH.